Tunnel Vision

The Life of a Copper Prospector
in the Nizina River Country

Mountains on all sides of me. Although I never saw big mountains before, they would always come to me in my dreams.

~Martin's Dream, circa 1973

THIS PAGE: Martin Radovan's trail followed the narrow shelf, running atop the greenstone for over a mile. Along the way, Martin faced numerous dangers, including falling rocks and ice from above, and a two thousand-foot drop descending to the unnamed glacier below. Courtesy of Jim Edwards.
RIGHT: Detail of copper stains at Binocular. Geneva-Pacific Collection, National Park Service.

Tunnel Vision

The Life of a Copper Prospector
in the Nizina River Country

Katherine Ringsmuth
The National Park Service
2012

Radovan's Cache.
Sketch by Nichole Mikesh,
National Park Service, 2007.

Table of Contents

Acknowledgements ix

Remembering Martin:
Foreword by Jim Edwards xv

A Life Lived in the "Land of Hope," an Introduction xvii

Marion Radovanovich Comes to America, 1900-1911 1

Augusta Louise Iverson:
From Norway to the Pacific Northwest, 1879-1911 9

Gold, Copper, and Love:
Life in Early Blackburn and McCarthy, 1912-1919 19

Martin and Augusta at Dan Creek, 1920-1931 25

The Prospector and the Impossible Prospect at Glacier Creek, 1929-1944 39

The Lone Prospector:
Life after "Gussie," 1944-1951 53

Business Deals and Family Reunions, 1951-1969 65

The Making of a Legend:
Martin's Final Years in the Nizina Country, 1970-1975 81

Tunnel Vision:
A Prospector's Legacy 93

Postscript 102

Afterword:
By NPS Historian Logan Hovis 103

Works Cited 104

Endnotes 110

Mountains and rivers shape the Nizina Country landscape.
Photograph by Samson Ferreira, National Park Service, 2007

Binocular is a secret, and mystery, to all but one man and I am that man!

~Martin Radovan
Martin's Dream, circa 1973

Photo by Mohylek, 2006.

Acknowledgements

The explorer is actually one who "seeks discoveries." He is not simply and solely the "discoverer." Instead the accent is upon process and activity, with advances in knowledge simply fortunate though expected incidents along the way. It is likewise not casual. It is purposeful. It is the seeking. It is one form of the learning process itself, and...it was often a branch of science which resulted in a discovery at a place trod many times over by previous generations of explorers bent on other missions in days gone by.

~William H. Goetzmann
Explorations and Empire: The Explorer and the Scientist in Winning the West

In summer 2010, the National Park Service, through its Abandoned Mine Lands program with funding from the American Recovery and Reinvestment Act, initiated the complex process of closing dangerous mines at Radovan Gulch, located in Wrangell-St. Elias National Park and Preserve. Before NPS personnel could begin sealing adits, the agency first had to comply with the National Historic Preservation Act and determine if the properties were eligible for listing on the National Register of Historic Places. After fieldwork and archival research, an interdisciplinary team determined that the camps, prospects, artifacts, roads and trails at Radovan Gulch maintained historical integrity, and were historically significant on a local level. But this story went far beyond compliance. Together, the historic properties, placed in context by numerous historic records, formed a remarkable time capsule of the enduring life and work of copper prospector, Martin Radovan. *Tunnel Vision: the Life of a Copper Prospector in the Nizina River Country* tells his story.

The completion of this book was, in no way, achieved alone. Several people must be recognized for their assistance. I must first acknowledge members of Martin Radovan's extended family, particularly, his great nephew, Aric Morton, and his niece, Katherine Cesare. Both were instrumental in providing information about Martin's early life and family background. Thanks must also go to Michael Magliari, Professor of

ABOVE: Jim Edwards at Radovan Gulch in what Martin called the "coyote hole," circa 1961. Courtesy of Jim Edwards.

Acknowledgements

History at Chico State University, and graduate student, Joshua Knudsen, for their handling of Martin Radovan's private collection, which Martin's family graciously provided for NPS use. Due to their combined efforts, many of the photographs appearing in this book are being viewed by the public for the first time.

Thanks must also extend to Emily Aiken Campbell, whose parents, Calvin and Viola Aiken, worked with Martin in the 1950s, and served as Martin's surrogate family until his permanent departure from Alaska in 1975. Over the years Emily had kept many of Martin's personal writings and records. These items were returned to Martin's family in California, and eventually made available for this publication. My gratitude must also go to Gary Green, who worked for Martin in the early 1970s. Both Emily and Gary gave me their time, sharing with me their fond memories of Martin. McCarthy residents Rick and Bonnie Kenyon provided articles and photographs from previous issues of their locally-run newspaper, *Wrangell St. Elias News* (WSEN), including one of the few known photographs of Augusta Radovan. Staff, employees and volunteers from Valdez Parks and Recreation, the Valdez Museum, the Cordova Museum, and the McCarthy Museum must also be recognized for their helpful dedication to and invaluable knowledge of the area's local history. My appreciation also goes out to the many people of McCarthy who expressed interest in and showed support for this history project.

Thanks to Norwegian genealogy researcher Kate Norby, Norwegian author Torbjorn Greipsland, the Scandinavian Club of Hawaii, the Hawaiian Historical Society, the Maui Historical Society, the Alexander & Baldwin Sugar Museum, King County Records office in Seattle, and Washington State's Division of Archives and Records Management for helping to reconstruct Augusta Radovan's early family life in Norway, Hawaii, and the Pacific Northwest.

Several National Park Service employees provided their time and expertise to the project. Geoffrey Bleakley, Danny Rosenkrans, Samson Ferreira, Mark Rollins, Janet Clemens, Linda Stromquist, Sarah Venator, and Ted Birkidal should all be recognized for their significant contributions in making this book a reality. Gloria Collins brought clarity to the biography with her editorial eye, and layout designer Francis Broderick made Martin's story come alive on the page.

Enormous recognition must also go to my colleague, Daniel Trepal, whose support on this project was instrumental in its realization. As my archeological counterpart, Dan provided important insights about the complex, and material-rich world of mining. Dan's expertise helped to determine Radovan Gulch Historic District as eligible for listing on the National Register of Historic Places. He created all the maps for the publication, read numerous drafts, and served as the all-important "sounding board" for my many historic theories, making sure that they were, indeed, historically sound. Through countless conversations, Dan helped me to better understand the significance of Martin's prospecting lifeway at Radovan Gulch, and contributed greatly to the narrative. Most importantly, Dan helped me to make sense of the so-called "junk" Martin and the other mining operators utilized, and in doing so, provided meaning for those items that otherwise would have been lost to time and history.

I must also thank Logan Hovis, NPS historian, whose expertise in mining history and knowledge of the Nizina River country made him the perfect project manager. It was Logan who first recognized the historical significance of Martin and Augusta, for they typify the forgotten prospectors of the Nizina country, who labored their entire lives in the shadow of Kennecott Mine. He believed that the lives of Martin and Augusta, as well as the historic properties associated with the couple, told a much larger story that needed to be shared with today's Alaskans and preserved for future generations. Thank you, Logan, for selecting me to write about these two extraordinary people.

Acknowledgements

Finally, I want to thank James "Jim" Edwards, who not only provided numerous personal photographs and memories of Martin, but shared his own life story with me, and in the process, became a great friend. Getting to know Jim throughout the project's duration has given me my own "wow experience," and like Martin and Augusta, I will never forget him.

NPS Historian Logan Hovis at Kennecott. Photograph by Katherine Ringsmuth, National Park Service, 2010.

To Augusta Radovan and all women who have shaped the history of the McCarthy area by following their own hopes and dreams.

Tunnel vision (also known as "Kalnienk Vision") is a disease of the eye indicated by the loss of peripheral vision. The resulting field of view is constricted and circular, as if looking looking out from inside a tunnel.

Martin's sunglasses. Martin Radovan Private Collection.

Remembering Martin: Foreword by Jim Edwards

IN GETTING TO KNOW VARIOUS PEOPLE THROUGH MY LIFE, those who most left me with a lasting feeling of "WOW, that was a great experience" were those who had lived or achieved something really special. Money or popularity had nothing to do with it. If a person's main focus was to accumulate wealth, my respect and interest dropped rapidly.

In my list of memorable life experiences, my friendship with Martin Radovan is near the top. For two summers (1955 and 1956) I worked for Bear Creek Mining, a subsidiary of Kennecott, exploring for new mineral deposits. I and a geologist worked for two summers from Martin's camp at Glacier Creek. Then, flying out to see Martin at Radovan Gulch over the next decade, I got to appreciate his mostly solo achievements. A particularly innovative achievement that stands out in my mind was how Martin, in order to access his cabin, built a hand-tram across Glacier Creek, tightening the cable by himself using only a pit, boulders, and gravity.

Another memory of Martin was his work at an extremely dangerous area in the gulch—a sixty degree chute, 4,000-feet high, where falling rocks and snowslides were commonplace. Near the bottom of the chute, a season of snow fall and melt had formed a treacherous *bergschrund*—a deep crevasse that if one fell in, it would be nearly impossible to get out. One day while prospecting in the area, Martin found a significant ore sample at a difficult place in the slide. Aware of the darkening skies, Martin, instead of taking the long way back to camp, deliberately slid down the last 100 feet of the 4,000-foot chute and with mounting speed, JUMPED the *bergschrund*! Although he cleared the crevasse, his momentum caused him to tumble head over heels and he lost the sample. Martin spent the rest of his life looking for the spot he found that sample.

This feat was especially impressive to me later, when I, myself, had to cross the *bergschrund* at Martin's site in 1955 and 1956. Not only was getting to Martin's tunnels dangerous, but we worked in the old way, with a

ABOVE: Jim Edwards and Norman Lutz surveying Radovan Gulch for the Bear Creek Mining Co. in 1955. Note the 4,000 ft. chute in the background. Courtesy of Jim Edwards.

Foreword: Remembering Martin

"single-jack" and rock point, and dynamite. During this summer's work, geologist Norm Lutz actually mapped the largest of Martin's sixteen tunnels to scale. It measured 125 feet of length. While working in that tunnel you had to be careful to get out of the hole before lighting the fuse, or you become a bullet. Moreover, the entry hole (called a coyote hole by Martin) usually closed itself up during your time in it, due to frequent slides of yet more snow.

In the summer months, I worked my way along the contact, and climbed up to the "Binocular Prospect," just as Martin first accomplished in 1929. When geologists arrived to inspect the site, Martin made numerous climbs to the prospect with supplies for their safety. These top geologist climbers, however, refused to ascend Binocular, despite having modern cleated boots and pitoned rope hand holds, put there by Martin. Working my way along that ten-inch wide ledge of loose rock, half way up a 4000-foot cliff, gave me much admiration for Martin, who climbed the trail in his old rubber shoe-pacs. Once, after several trips, I noticed, perched on top of a 15-foot high slab of vertical rock, a full sized cotton mattress, where Martin may have slept while working this site. Don't roll around in your sleep, ha!

That first spring I worked at Radovan Gulch, I lived at Martin's camp. Martin would fix breakfast for us 25 year olds. A day's work started with a four-mile climb to the base of the slide on snowshoes. Then we climbed on foot the additional 500 feet, (a total of about 2500 feet of altitude gain) up to the sixty degree slide against a descending breeze of -30 degree F, and pumped up a gas stove for coffee to warm up. Martin put away the breakfast dishes, prepared a meal for evening, and then climbed up and joined us to continue his tunnel work. Martin was 75 years old. By the time I had reached 75 years of age, I fully appreciated Martin's determination. But at the time, Martin didn't view his work as somehow extraordinary. He simply considered his work in the gulch the normal course of his life.

Over the years, seeing the warmth in his eyes as he showed me pictures of feeding the birds and his "Bootsie," a fox that took up residence with Martin in his cabin, and his sadness when he (rarely) mentioned his life with Augusta, gave me a clear view of this truly exceptional person I had come to know. Even though Martin never got rich, he had truly achieved something special in his life. Yes, my friendship with Martin Radovan stands out as a "WOW" experience, and is a reason to never forget him.

Jim Edwards
McCarthy, Alaska
July 27, 2011

Jim Edwards at his home in McCarthy, Alaska. Photograph by Katherine Ringsmuth, National Park Service, 2010.

A Life Lived in the "Land of Hope": An Introduction

Mountains, on all sides of me. Although I never saw big mountains before, they would always come to me in my dreams.

~Martin Radovan
Martin's Dream

In a 1912 article for *Scribner's Magazine,* Dora Keen, the first mountaineer to ascend Mount Blackburn, described the Alaskan prospectors she had encountered while visiting the Nizina country the previous year. "His motto is 'Never stuck…'" she wrote, "…His is the land of hope. He is always 'going to make a strike next year, sure,' therefore always ready to endure and to smile, whatever happens."[1] Had she met Martin Radovan, she would have described the prospector and his unyielding faith in his prospects perfectly. Martin came to Alaska following a dream: "Arriving in New York, then step by step to Alaska…," recalled an aging Martin, "…I came half way round the world to the mountains of my dreams." Whether crossing oceans and continents, surmounting glaciers and cliffs, or befriending the local wildlife, Martin Radovan never doubted there was copper to be found deep within the mountains of the Nizina River Country, a place that, after a lifetime of prospecting, became his "land of hope."

Martin spent his entire adult life searching for copper in the Nizina Mining District in the Chitina copper belt, located in the shadow of the Wrangell Mountains in eastern Alaska. The saga of copper and its pursuit by humans is, of course, far-reaching and ancient. With the advent of metallurgy five thousand years ago, people began to alloy copper with tin, thus initiating one of the major "ages" of human history—the Bronze Age. The Roman discovery of a new copper alloy, brass, caused the productivity of coppersmiths to soar throughout antiquity. During the Renaissance, notable sculptors worked with bronze, and painters commonly used thin sheets of copper as their canvases. It is well known that Watt's steam engine, which ushered in the Industrial Revolution, depended largely on iron and coal. Yet copper also helped pave the road to modernity with

ABOVE: Nikolai Butte at Dan Creek, date unknown. Photograph by Martin Radovan. Martin Radovan Private Collection.

A Life Lived in the "Land of Hope": An Introduction

attributes such as durability and resistance to corrosion, which made it the choice metal for steam pipes, plumbing, automobile radiators, and other heat exchange devices. The Statue of Liberty, dedicated to the United States by France in 1886, is made of copper. But it was Edison's invention of the incandescent light bulb in 1879 and the subsequent development of electrical power that revolutionized the global demand for copper.

Alaska Natives of the Wrangell Mountains had long used the copper found in their streams, fashioning the nuggets into arrowheads, cooking utensils, and knives. Copper was an important article of trade, with intertribal commerce extending as far south as the Queen Charlotte Islands in Canada. Coastal Natives told early explorers that the copper had come from a rugged inland area to the north. Tales of a "copper mountain" provoked tall tales among the early traders and pioneers, but no real attempt was made to find the deposits until Lt. Henry Allen's expedition in 1885.[2] While his party was exploring the Chitina River region, Allen sought a meeting with Chief Nicolai, the head chief of the Copper River Ahtna, at his hunting camp on Dan Creek. Allen and his men were starving. In order to save his troops, Allen sought assistance from the local Native people. Nicolai gave Allen a portion of his people's meager food and provisions, and thus rescued the expedition.[3] Nicolai also showed Allen the Ahtnas' copper utensils and knives, and may even have shown Allen the source of the native copper—Nicolai's famed "Copper Mine."[4]

Annual flooding of the Copper River often washed out the Copper River & Northwest Railway at Chitina, Alaska between 1911 and 1938. Courtesy of Emily Aiken Campbell.

Fourteen years after the Nicolai meeting at Dan Creek, William S. Abercrombie was sent into the region to construct a safe military trail into the interior in order to support the increasing numbers of miners heading for the Klondike. Abercrombie blazed a rugged new trail from Valdez through the mountains over Thompson Pass and

A Life Lived in the "Land of Hope": An Introduction

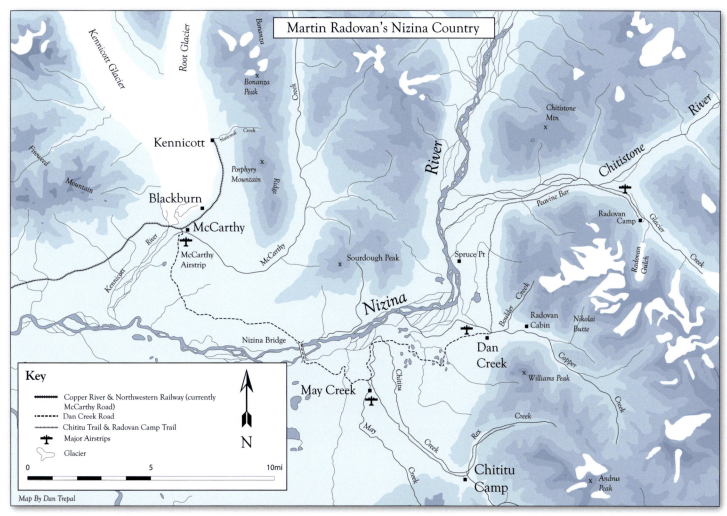

Martin Radovan's Nizina Country. Map by Daniel Trepal, National Park Service.

made the headwaters of the Copper River relatively accessible for the first time. Not surprisingly, a procession of prospectors came in the wake of federal road-building, and as historian M. J. Kirchhoff writes, "The legend of Lt. Henry Allen's Nikolai Mine was vivid in their minds."[5]

The rising economic interest in copper prompted Abercrombie to send Oscar Rohn up the Chitina River also in the summer of 1899. While struggling up the Chitina, Rohn came across the camp of a prospector named James McCarthy. McCarthy lent Rohn some of his surplus horses and supplies, and, in return, Rohn named a creek farther up the river for McCarthy. He also named the nearby glacier after Robert Kennicott, an early Alaskan explorer. Rohn was the first explorer to describe in detail the McCarthy and Kennicott area. He recorded geological formations, noted the mineralization in the area, and wrote that he had found slivers of copper ore called "copper floats" in the gravel of McCarthy Creek.[6]

Rohn's investigations laid the foundation for many subsequent geological surveys and mineral discoveries in the Nizina district. Like previous government expeditions, Rohn benefitted from the company of prospectors and Natives, who already had acquired working knowledge of routes and conditions found in the Nizina country, as

Prospectors like Martin Radovan considered the Nizina Country a "land of hope."
Photograph by Samson Ferreira, National Park Service, 2007.

A Life Lived in the "Land of Hope": An Introduction

well as locations of gold-bearing placers and copper-bearing lodes. Rohn made his findings public in 1899. A year later, prospectors Clarence Warner and Jack Smith discovered Kennecott's[7] world-famous Bonanza copper deposit along a depositional contact zone, where the light-gray marine rocks of the Chitistone Limestone cap the distinctive maroon-colored slopes of the Nikolai Greenstone, a formation that dominates much of the visual landscape south of the Wrangell Mountains. It seemed that Martin Radovan picked a good time to begin his story as a copper prospector in the Nizina River Country.

In pursuit of a dream, nineteen-year-old Martin Radovan departed his home town of Žrnovo, Croatia, an Austrian province of the Austro-Hungarian Empire, for the United States in 1900, the same year of the Bonanza strike a half a world away. When he arrived at Ellis Island, his surname, "Radovanovich," was changed to "Radovan." He gained railroad experience in New Jersey and in California, but after the 1906 earthquake that leveled much of San Francisco, Martin moved to Seattle. It was in the Pacific Northwest where Martin learned of a railway being constructed into the Interior of Alaska by J. P. Morgan and the Guggenheim family.

J.P. Morgan and the Guggenheims provided the financial backing for the Kennecott Copper Company. Together they formed the Alaska Syndicate, which developed Kennecott's copper lodes, constructed the mill to process the ore, and built the Copper River & Northwestern Railway from Cordova to McCarthy. Courtesy of Jim Edwards.

The two titans of American business—J.P. Morgan and the Guggenheim brothers—were drawn to Alaska for one simple reason. By the early twentieth century, copper was the coveted metal made increasingly valuable by America's desire for electric power. With such influence and corporate power looming, claim to the Bonanza lode failed to remain in the hands of Warner and Smith. Through the wheeling and dealing efforts of Stephen Birch, mining claims were consolidated with the formation of the Kennecott Copper Company in 1906. Soon thereafter, Morgan and the Guggenheims, along with on-the-ground oversight by Birch, began development of the copper

A Life Lived in the "Land of Hope": An Introduction

lodes. They built a mill to process the ore, and commenced construction of the Copper River & Northwestern (CR & NW) Railway, the means by which these captains of industry would send their valuable copper from the heart of the rugged Wrangell Mountains to an insatiable outside market.

Martin arrived at the coastal terminus town of Cordova in 1908. Putting his railroad skills to good use, he quickly found work building the CR & NW Railway. After its completion in 1911, Martin took a job with a hydraulic mining company at Dan Creek, south of present day McCarthy, and began to prospect nearby creeks and benches for gold on his own. In the 1920s, Martin was attracted by a green-stained outcropping in a glacial cirque on Glacier Creek, a tributary of the Chitistone River. The presence of surface erosion indicated the leaching of copper. The prospect of copper, combined with the rich Bonanza Ridge discoveries, convinced Martin—and others—that a massive copper deposit lay deep within the weathering cliffs of the Chitistone Limestone, overlaying the rimming peaks of the gulch.

The geologic story of the Wrangell Mountains' greenstone and limestone deposits is fascinating in its own right. Both deposits originated thousands of miles away from Alaska, somewhere near the earth's equator.[8] However, they were made from entirely different geologic processes. The Nikolai Greenstone consists of basalts deposited by ancient lava flows approximately 250 to 200 million years ago during a period known as the Triassic. The Chitistone Limestone, on the other hand, was created by an evaporated oceanic tidal flat, forming about that same time. Geologists believe that the source of the rich ore deposits at the famed Kennecott mines was the Nikolai Greenstone. How copper was actually placed into the greenstone basalts remained a mystery for years.

The scientific community has known for a long time that copper is a basic building block of the universe, one of the ninety-two atomic elements which occur naturally on earth and from which all other substances are made.[9] However, a majority of scientists have come to agree in recent decades that most of the galaxy's copper was slowly fused in "supergiants," the biggest stars in the universe.[10] Both of the metals Martin sought in the Nizina district—gold and copper—were products of massive stars. The placer gold at Dan Creek and elsewhere was originally created during the intensely bright explosive moment in a dying star. But the copper of the Bonanza Ridge lodes and outcrops at Binocular, and in fact all the copper on earth, was forged over the course of millions of years in massive interstellar furnaces.[11]

The copper landscape of Wrangell Mountain was shaped millions of years ago when northward drifting tectonic plates containing alien rock collided and, slowly and incrementally, extended the ancient North American continental margin. Such geological forces built a mountain chain and, in the process, brought molten rock magma containing copper much closer to the surface. Water from the surface percolated down into the earth, dissolving the copper minerals from the magma. This superheated mineral-laden water was then driven back towards the surface, where it gradually worked its way into cracks and fissures in the rock above. When the water cooled, chalcocite, chalcopyrite, and other minerals were left behind, forming easily recognizable veins of minerals.[12]

Geologists believe that after the Chitistone Limestone was deposited millions of years ago, part of the copper ore was leached out of the Nikolai Greenstone by superheated water and deposited in favorable places in both the greenstone and the limestone.[13] Being more fractured, the limestone became the host to larger and richer deposits than the greenstone. This meant that, at the turn of the century when such deposits were being discovered, the U.S. Geological Survey (USGS) advised prospectors to look for copper veins in the so-called "contact zone," where the distinctly colored deposits meet.[14]

Under the direction of the federal government, USGS had cultivated with private investors a new field known as "economic geology." This marked the end of geological pioneering in the Wrangell Mountains and instituted more

A Life Lived in the "Land of Hope": An Introduction

systematic investigations of the region's geological environment and mineral resources. As early as 1905, geologic maps and reports of mining districts began to serve as treasure maps and "how-to" manuals for miners. Fred H. Moffit and his USGS colleagues who focused on the southern flank of the Wrangell Mountains recognized early on that the copper was most likely found near the visually distinct greenstone/limestone contact and advised prospectors to begin exploring there:

> *The most important conclusion bearing on the economic geology here presented is the fact that the copper-ore bodies appear to occur chiefly along a system of cross fractures which are at approximately right angles to the greenstone-limestone contact. These fractures occur along well-defined faults, at least one of which has been traced for a long distance. This may apply to the entire Chitina district find and is worthy of consideration by the prospector.*[15]

Once word of where to search got out, Martin Radovan, like nearly all the copper prospectors working the Nizina district, began to scrutinize every accessible linear foot of the contact zone.

Martin's early claim to fame came with his "conquest" of the Binocular Prospect, the copper-stained outcrop above the greenstone-limestone contact on the face of a cliff overlooking a large, glacier-filled cirque on the south side of the Glacier Creek drainage, a cirque that was later named Radovan Gulch. USGS experts had known about the outcrop and had studied it—through binoculars—since the turn of the century. However, the vertical face of the cirque wall and the location of the outcrop over 3,000 feet up prevented geologists from gaining detailed inspection and sampling. By the mid-1920s, the Binocular outcrop had even perked the interests of the giant Kennecott Copper Corporation, which at the time sought to extend its operational life by exploring for other mining opportunities in the Nizina district. In 1929, the company took an option on a nearby prospect and that same year sent European mountain climbers to try to reach Binocular. After a summer of attempts, these skillful climbers failed to reach the contact and obtain samples for Kennecott.

Martin, however, managed to do what the experts could not. He reached the outcrop by following a precipitous route along the cliff wall and built a stair-step trail, only one-foot wide at places, toward the contact zone. At a point two hundred feet below the outcrop, he scaled the face of the cliff, using ropes and steel spikes driven into the rock crevices. Martin staked some thirty claims over the next two years. Although Kennecott never optioned or leased his claims, Martin nevertheless gained local respect and notoriety for besting the Kennecott Copper Corporation and beating their hired expert climbers to the copper-stained outcrops, and, perhaps most important of all, he became a local legend for his death-defying route that allowed him to access the Binocular Prospect in the first place.

Supporting Martin in his early mining endeavors was his wife, Augusta Louise Iverson, a person of great significance in Martin's life. Somehow Martin—a prospector who spent more time in a tunnel than in town—caught the attention of a Norwegian bookkeeper who worked at the Kennecott milltown. Martin and Augusta were married by the Justice of the Peace in McCarthy in 1914. Moving seasonally between the cabin at Dan Creek and the camp at Glacier Creek, she made a life with him in the Nizina country for three decades.

Augusta contributed to Martin's legendary life in notable ways. Not only did Augusta assist Martin with his mining ambitions, but when she was a child, Augusta's family participated in a little-known Scandinavian migration to the Hawaiian Islands in 1880. This reflected the experience of European immigrants who followed pathways to America via the Pacific. Her personal reasons for coming to Alaska directly challenge outdated interpretations of female pioneers who hesitantly moved West to follow the men in their lives—the so-called "reluctant pioneers." In McCarthy, Augusta socialized with important figures in the Woman's Christian Temperance Movement. She

A Life Lived in the "Land of Hope": An Introduction

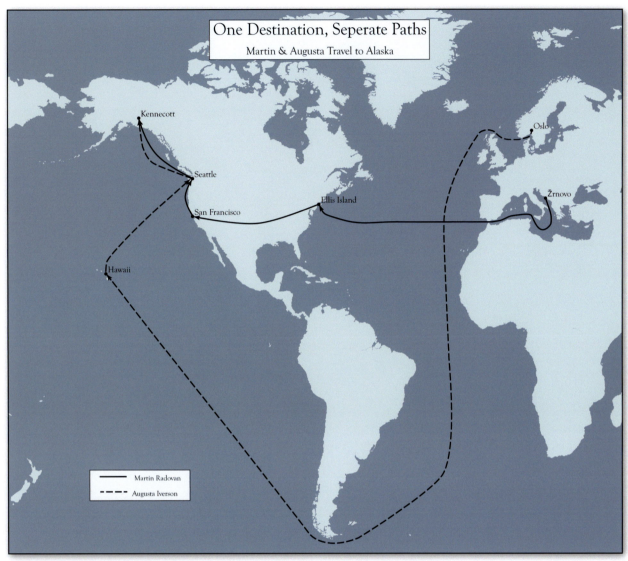

One Destination, Separate Paths. Map by Daniel Trepal, National Park Service.

was a bookkeeper at Kennecott, she was a notary and assistant postmistress at Dan Creek, and she was part of the first generation of female jurors in Cordova; most significantly, Augusta's experience in the Nizina district provides insight into the social organization of mining societies. As defined by the reciprocal nature of their marriage, Martin and Augusta's relationship serves as a case study on the individual lives of men and women and the history they made together. Like Martin, Augusta's story has also contributed to local mythology, for the mystery surrounding her death has continued to link her with Radovan Gulch, and interestingly, she may be the only Radovan still there.

Augusta's life was cut short in 1944 when she was sixty-five years old. But Martin, for the next thirty years, continued his search for copper in the cirque which bears his name. Besides the Binocular Prospect, he discovered and staked two others, Low-Contact and the Greenstone, and built a substantial camp on the banks of Glacier Creek near the mouth of Radovan Gulch. Alone and unaided, Martin built a tram that allowed him to cross Glacier Creek to his creekside camp. When he was not tunneling into the limestone, Martin passed time by feeding

A Life Lived in the "Land of Hope": An Introduction

A chair found in Martin's cabin at Glacier Creek during a survey of the site in 2010. Photograph by Daniel Trepal, National Park Service.

the local wildlife, an activity that brought him much comfort after "Gussie" died. In 1948, Martin filed twelve claims at Radovan Gulch, many of which were named after things he cherished most: his pet fox "Boots," the grey jays he called "Ki-Ki" birds, a bear he called "Pongo Boy," and his wife and partner of thirty years, "Augusta."

By a twist of fate, Martin was reunited with his long-lost brother, Jack Radovich of Delano, California, in 1951. Jack, a wealthy vineyard owner, flew to Glacier in hopes of reuniting with his brother, Martin, whom he had not seen in fifty years. Jack wanted his sourdough brother to return with him to Delano, but the family reunion did not deter Martin from his mining aspirations. As Martin recalled, "I had some good claims and was preparing for the winter."[16] All too aware that he needed a company with the capital and technology to develop his prospects, Martin remained at Glacier Creek, persistently working his claims and marketing the prospects to outside interests.

After a string of disappointing leases and business arrangements between the 1950s and the late 1960s, a geological and geophysical exploration company, the Geneva-Pacific Corporation, purchased Martin's prospects in the early 1970s, giving Martin hope that the Binocular Prospect would finally be mined and his life work validated. In 1974, at age ninety-two, Martin left Alaska to spend time with his brother, Jack, in Delano. The following spring, Geneva-Pacific's professional geologists finally reached the Binocular Prospect using a helicopter. The geologists, awed by Martin's lifelong feats, took samples and returned to California. But before the company's findings were reported, Martin died.

A Life Lived in the "Land of Hope": An Introduction

Martin's Glacier Creek Cabin in July, 2010. Photograph by Daniel Trepal, National Park Service.

Had any of his claims proved to be substantial at depth, Martin, or at least his extended family, would have been rich. Of course, this was not to be Martin's fate. Martin never found what he believed was a copper mountain at Radovan Gulch. But what Martin did unearth over the years, after a lifetime of hard work, love, and undaunted faith, is told in *Tunnel Vision: The Life of a Copper Prospector in the Nizina River Country*. Martin Radovan lived and worked in the Nizina Mining District for nearly seventy years. His camp at Glacier Creek served as a staging area for mineral exploration of the nearby gulch until the late 1970s. In many ways, Martin was one of the hundreds of individuals whom National Park Service historian Geoffrey Bleakley calls "the forgotten prospectors," those who worked throughout the Wrangell Mountain region in the shadow of the corporate giant, the Kennecott Copper Corporation.[17]

Still, unlike many of these so-called forgotten prospectors, Martin Radovan is unique because he stayed. He therefore stands out from this group and establishes himself as a person significant in our past through his long career and local notoriety as a daring and persistent prospector at Radovan Gulch. For residents of the Nizina country, Martin is clearly a person "significant in THEIR past." As a National Park Service archeologist remarked, "the prospect and the prospector became part of the local legend."[18]

A Life Lived in the "Land of Hope": An Introduction

Although Martin's Glacier Creek camp is deteriorating at a rapid rate, the structures that remain reflect nearly a half century of his presence there, and collectively, the camps, prospects, roads and trails, and artifacts left behind continue to tell an amazing story of a prospector and his seventy-year relationship with a place. Together, the historic properties form a remarkable time capsule of the life and times of a prospector in the Nizina Mining District. Thus, instead of disappointment, Martin Radovan, the undaunted prospector, lived an important life—always ready to endure and to smile—in a place that can only be described as his "land of hope."

"Mount Blackburn, Alaska, 16,140 feet high." P.S. Hunt created the postcard in 1911, the same year the CR&NW Railroad was completed and Dora Keen attempted to climb the peak. (Image expanded digitally to fit page.)

Marion Radovanovich Comes to America
1900–1911

Time to go, it must be admitted. At the thought of having to bid good-by, to all, and everything I ever had, hard for me, to leave home for the first time. We stood, and looked at one another, crying.

~Martin Radovan
Martin's Dream

MARION[19] FRANK RADOVANOVICH WAS BORN ON OCTOBER 13, 1882[20] IN ŽRNOVO, CROATIA, an Austrian province of the Austro-Hungarian Empire.[21] Martin's father, Marin Radovanovich, and his mother, Jaka Segedin Radovanovich, were both from the island of Korcula, located off the Dalmatian Coast in the Adriatic Sea.[22] At the age of eighteen, Martin immigrated to the United States to find work and allegedly to avoid conscription into the Imperial Austrian Army.[23] Years later, Martin recalled a story that illustrates the influence his parents had on his decision to leave his Mediterranean island:

One day I asked my father how big is the world? He said, too big for you to think about. But how big is it? I insisted. If you really like to know, [said his father] this Island is thirty miles long, when you get to the end of it, that is the end for you, until you get to be a man, now get [to be] that man. The next day I asked mother, how big is the world mama? Very big my boy, there is no end to it, if you start to walk today, and live to be a hundred years old, if you don't use your head, you get no place. But mom we don't walk on our heads. I know that son, but by using your head you will save lots [of] walking.[24]

A combination of romantic adventure, economic need, and the reality of war probably convinced Martin to leave Korcula. He departed on "June first nineteen hundred" on what he described later as a very sad day.[25]

ABOVE: Found among Martin's personal items was a lunch menu from the Alaska Steamship Company. On the front cover of the menu is a photograph of Childs Glacier on which Martin scribbled, "Bridge Mile 49, ¼ mile up." Martin Radovan Private Collection.

S.S. YUKON

H. ANDERSEN, Lieut.-Commander U.S.N.R.
Commanding

Tuesday May 24, 1932

LUNCH

Green Onions and Radishes   Spiced Beets   Dill Pickle

Vermicelli Broth   Beef Bouillon

Broiled Sablefish Anchovy Butter

Grilled Luncheon Steak Bordelaise Sauce

Curried Veal with Rice

Wheat Pancake with Honey

Boiled Potatoes   Baked Southern Yams

COLD BUFFET

Prime Ribs of Beef with Horseradish

Corned Beef   Blood Sausage

Roast Leg of Lamb   Kippered Salmon

Potato Salad Served with Cold Buffet Orders

Cumberland Salad   Italian Dressing

Grape Nut Custard Pudding   Cream Sauce

Banana Cream Pie   Lime Jell-O   Whipped Cream   Queen Cakes

Preserved Pears   Fresh Fruit in Season

American Cottage or Pimento Cheese

Coffee   Cocoa   Postum   Butter Milk   Fresh Milk

Black or Green Tea

ARTHUR PAYNE, *Chief Steward*

Envelopes for Mailing may be Obtained from Waiter

Please Refrain from Smoking in the Dining Room

THE ALASKA LINE

Marion Radovanovich Comes to America

Martin left his large extended family, boarded a boat, and steamed into New Jersey Harbor, arriving at Ellis Island on July 1, 1900.[26] While passing into the United States, Martin's name, like so many European immigrants, was transliterated—"Radovanovich" was shortened to "Radovan."

The young and hard-working Martin Radovan quickly found employment on the East Coast. He first worked for the American Pencil Company in Hoboken, New Jersey, for two years; then he found a job on the Erie Railroad Float Bridge as a night-crew foreman until he was laid off due to an injury.[27] Martin later recalled, "On leaving my home in Austria I was just a boy, young and awkward, bashful, from the country, with [my] mind slowly ripening in its rough husk gathering gear…I moved from place to place, scouring knowledge in order to use it, and by using it absolutely my own, [I gained] capacity for more."[28]

Picking up occupational know-how and putting it to use appears to be precisely what Martin did in those early years. The desire to learn more about the railroad business (presumably sparked while working on the Erie Railroad Float Bridge, a float bridge that delivered rail cars to destinations in New York by barge) drew Martin across the country to San Francisco, where he worked for the Southern Pacific Railway shops.[29] Martin's stay in California, however, was brief. He was living across the bay in Oakland during the 1906 earthquake, which ignited a fire that destroyed much of San Francisco.[30] Martin later recalled that he "could read the paper by the light of the fire in the City."[31] Martin told his niece, Katherine Cesare, that he "decided to leave San Francisco on the first boat he could book passage…the boat was going to Seattle."[32] Martin traveled first to Portland and then to Seattle via steamship.[33]

Apparently, Martin's time in the Pacific Northwest was also short. He quickly put his railroad skills to good use and, in 1907, decided in his words "to pursue advertisements he'd seen to work on the Cordova and Northwestern

ABOVE: Building Railroad in Woods Canyon, Alaska, circa 1910. Courtesy of Geoff Bleakley, Copper Center, Alaska.
LEFT: Martin saved this lunch menu from the Alaska Steamship Company's Alaska Line, perhaps as a souvenir of a trip to Alaska in 1908. Martin Radovan Private Collection.

The 1910 U.S. Census found Martin Radovan working in Woods Canyon. "C.R. & N.W. RY. Mile 125, August 27, 1910." Courtesy of Geoff Bleakley, Copper Center, Alaska.

Marion Radovanovich Comes to America

Railway work crews stack limestone, forming a foundation for the tracks at Woods Canyon. This was typical work for Martin. Courtesy of Geoff Bleakley, Copper Center, Alaska.

Railroad in Alaska."[34] The pay was advertised at $3 a day, much more than he had ever made in his life.[35] Martin arrived at Cordova, Alaska, on October 9, 1908, and quickly found work for the Katalla Company, the contractor building the Copper River & Northwestern Railway.[36] Celebrated as an engineering feat, the railway line cost nearly $25 million to build. Supporting the line were two American business giants: financier J.P. Morgan and the Guggenheims, a family of industrialists who made its fortune in the mining and smelting industry.

Rousing the investment interests of Morgan and the Guggenheims were the lobbying efforts of Stephen Birch, a mining engineer convinced of the economic potential of a copper ore deposit, aptly named Bonanza, discovered in the limestone and greenstone contact near the Kennicott Glacier in 1901. Although mining engineers reported that the ore bodies at Bonanza were extraordinarily rich, the claims lay two hundred miles from the coast, in some of the most rugged terrain in Alaska. With only shoddy winter trails and impossible summer trails on which to travel and carry supplies, an enormous amount of financial support was needed to develop the Bonanza deposit and make it profitable.[37]

Initially, Birch had joined the thirteen-member party, known as the McClellan Group, who originally staked the Bonanza claims. After seeing the ore deposit first hand, however, Birch began to buy out the individual shareholders, acting on behalf of Norman Schultz and Henry O. Havemeyer, sugar baron and Birch's childhood friend.[38] Once Birch acquired the majority of the shares in the McClellan Party, he formed the Alaska Copper and Coal Company in order to manage the claims on behalf of his backers. But after the potential worth of the mine became public, Birch found himself in court, defending his legal title to the claims. In a gesture that reflected his confidence for legal victory, as well as his belief in the prospect, Birch, while still in litigation, invested $400,000 in development work at Bonanza.[39] In 1902, he built the first structure at the Kennecott Mill site, a log cabin at National Creek, and broke a trail up the mountainside to the green outcropping.[40]

But to fully develop Bonanza's copper Birch's investment only scratched the surface. Knowing he still needed to raise enormous capital, Birch proceeded to lobby two of the biggest players in American business, J. P. Morgan and the Guggenheims. Meanwhile, Birch's Alaska Copper and Coal Company prevailed in the court of Alaskan judge James Wickersham, defeating the law suits filed against him.[41] In 1906, Birch won over his potential investors, merging the financial interests of the J.P. Morgans with the mining and smelting interests of the Guggenheims. Jointly, they formed the Alaska Syndicate, which acquired a 40 percent interest in the newly formed Kennecott Copper Mines Company and made Birch the company manager.[42] Building a transportation system that could haul building supplies and machinery to the mine site and copper ore out to national markets was the Syndicate's first priority.[43]

What made the Syndicate's gamble on the Bonanza deposit worthwhile was America's transition to electrical power, which tremendously increased the market's demand for copper by the end of the nineteenth century. In 1879,

Marion Radovanovich Comes to America

"Railroad Completed to the Copper Belt." *The Chitina Leader*, April 1, 1911.

Thomas Edison perfected the long-lasting incandescent light bulb, an invention that revolutionized American society and way of life.[44] Historian Timothy J. LeCain notes that what was equally striking about the invention was that Edison had to "plug it in," for conducting electricity to Edison's light bulb was heavy copper wire.[45] From that day on, copper was the metal of choice to serve the growing demands of national electrification.[46]

Once completed, the Syndicate's CR & NW Railway ferried in the rush of investors, developers, suppliers, and some late-comer copper miners to the Nizina district. Spanning a distance of 192 miles from the site of the tremendous, yet practically inaccessible, Bonanza deposit in the Wrangell Mountains to the coastal town of Cordova, the railway overcame nearly impossible obstacles. Martin Radovan recalled that in order to get the ore to market, a railroad had to "cross the mossy swamps of the broad river delta and pass for miles over the solid ice of the great coastal glaciers, and then carve its way through the rocky cliffs of the lower canyon."[47] In four years, railroad crews chiseled roadbed from sheer rock, laid track on a moving glacier, and bridged the immense Copper River.[48] In 1911, Alfred H. Brooks, head of the U.S. Geological Survey in Alaska, called the completion of the CR & NW Railway "the most important advance made in the history of Alaska transportation since steamboat service was established on the Yukon."[49]

Thus, the relatively high prices of copper, coupled with the country's so-called "copper famine," justified the enormous expense of over $35 million to develop the mine and transportation system. After two mis-starts, first at

Marion Radovanovich Comes to America

Valdez and then at Katella, construction of the railway began from the fishing town of Cordova in 1907. Martin Radovan was one of the thousands of laborers hired to construct the railway and was witness to the growth of Cordova, which in Martin's words, "sprung up, like a flower, in May of 1908."[50] Martin worked at a variety of positions, and later told a reporter that he had learned bridge building and some engineering while working on the railway. He labored for four years, long enough to see it completed in 1911.[51] He even received a patent in 1914 on an invention that would have prevented a train accident that he once witnessed. The invention, according to Martin, was a "plate placed at the ends of the ties designed to prevent the gapping caused by steel tracks laid in summer that tended to contract in the winter." Despite its practicality, the plate was never used.[52]

The U.S. Census found Martin working at the CR & NW's Woods Canyon railroad camp as a single laborer in the spring of 1910. Martin was not always forthcoming about his Croatian/Austrian heritage. He told the census recorder that his father came from France and mother from Bohemia.[53] There is no record of a "Martin F. Radovan" or "Radovanovich" passing through Ellis Island in 1900. He refused to declare his country of origin on his World War I Draft Registration Card,[54] and in 1920, he lied again, telling a census taker that he and his father

J.P. Hubrick lived in McCarthy between 1916 and 1930. He was known for his panoramic photographs of the Wrangell Mountains. This Hubrick postcard of the Kennicott Glacier was found among Martin's personal items. Martin Radovan Private Collection.

Marion Radovanovich Comes to America

Martin and Augusta likely met at the Kennicott milltown where they were both employed at the same time. Courtesy of Geoff Bleakley, Copper Center, Alaska.

were French.[55] Miners and prospectors are by nature secretive, but motivating Martin's dishonesty was probably the social and political upheaval plaguing his homeland during the first decades of the twentieth century. In Bosnia and Herzegovina, a neighboring Austrian province, a Bosnian Serb assassinated Archduke Franz Ferdinand, heir to the throne of the Austro-Hungarian Empire, in 1914. The assassination caused the Austro-Hungarian Empire to declare war on Serbia, becoming the catalyst for the outbreak of World War I. If Martin did in fact leave his home country to avoid conscription, then he would have indeed wanted to disassociate himself from the increasingly hostile Austrian Empire.

Moreover, Martin probably lied about his place of birth to avoid discrimination by his current countrymen. It makes sense that Martin would not want it known that he was from a country with which the United States was about to go to war. Furthermore, Martin was part of a massive wave of immigrants to the United States understood by many to be the "new immigrants," because unlike earlier immigrants who came primarily from northern and western Europe, the majority of these newcomers came from non-English speaking European countries, particularly southern and eastern Europe. The perception existed among many Americans that the newly arriving immigrants were somehow inferior to those who arrived earlier.

At the same time that Martin was making his way across the nation and to Alaska, an increasingly vocal group of politicians and Nativists began to demand restrictions on the immigration of the newest arrivals. In an attempt to preserve the ethnic character of the "old immigrants," the federal government passed laws and regulations such as the Chinese Exclusion Act and the Alien Contract Labor Law, and it instituted literacy tests. Such discriminatory activities peaked between 1921, with the passage of the Quota Laws, and 1924, with the passage of the National Origins Act. Thus, it is not surprising that Martin Radovan, a young immigrant from the Adriatic Coast, whose name had once been Radovanovich, chose to conceal his southern European roots and remain, if possible, invisible.[56]

Augusta Louise Iverson:
From Norway to the Pacific Northwest
1879–1911

Monday, 14 February: On the evening of this day, as fate would have it, we got to see land, Hawaii. The promised land. ... We anchored right by a little town, but we could hardly see it because of the palms and banana trees. Many natives came to look at us, and they probably thought we were some strange people.

~Nils Emil Aars, *Beta* passenger
Journal entry, February 14, 1881

MARTIN RADOVAN WAS NOT INVISIBLE TO EVERYONE. Somehow this brown-eyed, black-haired Croatian with a muscular build caught the attention of a pretty Norwegian bookkeeper who worked at the Kennecott mill town. Her name was Augusta Louise Iverson. Augusta's father was Johan Alfred Iversen,[57] the son of Iver Tonnesen. Johan was a mason from Oslo, Norway, who married Thora Laurette Fredrikke, daughter of Lars Nyrholm and also from Oslo, on October 31, 1879. Nine days before she married, Thora gave birth to a baby girl at Fodselstiftelsen (The Birth Institution) in Oslo. Three day later, on October 26, Thea Augusta Lovise was baptized. The family emigrated from Norway a year later.[58]

Norway, in the late nineteenth century, was in the midst of a depression. Unemployment was widespread throughout the country. The Iversons were most likely extremely poor and, in order to survive, joined other Norwegians in a mass migration to America. But unlike most Scandinavians who sailed to America by way of the Atlantic Coast, then traveled on to the Midwest, and for some, like Martin, the Pacific Coast, Augusta's family made it to the Pacific Northwest by way of a voyage to the Hawaiian Islands—a paid voyage that took them half way around the world to work on a sugar plantation on the island of Maui.[59]

ABOVE: The bark *Beta* sailed from Norway to Hawaii in 1880 with 400 passengers, many of whom were young families. Aboard were Johan and Thora Iverson with their infant daughter, Augusta. Courtesy of the Scandinavian Club of Hawaii.

Augusta Louise Iverson: From Norway to the Pacific Northwest

To attract hard-working help, local newspapers in Drammen, Tidende, and other towns throughout Norway printed the following message:

Saccharum officinarum, sugar cane. Illustration by Franz Eugen Köhler, from *Köhler's Medizinal-Pflanzen*, 1897.

Contracts with those who will go to the Sandwich Islands, are drawn up and signed on Wednesday, Sept 23, and the following days at the office of Hans P. Faye, at Drammen from 11 to 3 o'clock. The parties must be provided with good recommendations, and attestations for good and faultless behavior. Parties under obligation of military service, must bring release from service. Signature for minors must, to be valid, be confirmed by guardian. The conditions are now regulated, and thus fixed: Laborers over 20 years, 9 dollars; under 20 years, somewhat less, per month, with free board, or board-money and free lodging, families may bring two children with them. Free passage and board, which is not to be worked out afterwards.

On July 20, 1880, the Hawaii Bureau of Immigration authorized Captain Christian L'Orange to sail four hundred Norwegian passengers, mostly young married couples, on a four-month journey across the North Atlantic, around Cape Horn into the Pacific, and to the Hawaiian Islands.[60]

The bark *Beta* left Drammen, Norway, on October 27, 1880. According to the passenger list, Johan A. Iversen embarked with his wife and infant.[61] The voyage was long and arduous. The *Beta* was outfitted with bread, crackers, flour, salt-dried fish, a few live hogs, and fifty chickens—barely enough provisions for over four hundred passengers and crew members for several months. The passengers endured everything from rough seas and fires to melancholy and a bittersweet Christmas celebration as they passed Cape Horn. Nine children died of seasickness, malnutrition, or accident. One couple lost two young sons within two weeks of each other, and in the midst of great suffering, five babies were born.[62]

135	177	A. Fred	Larsen	m		
136	178	Andreas	Ericksen	m		
137	179	Chris	Christophersen	m		
138	180	Elise	Rasmussen	w		
139	181	Jonas	Olsen	m		
140	182	Johan M.	Knudsen	m		
141,1	183	Johan A.	Iversen	m	husband	
141,2	184			w	wife	
141,3	185				child	9/12
142,1	186	Johan A.	Henricksen	m	husband	
142,2	187			w	wife	
142,3	188				child	

Detail: *Beta* passenger list showing the Iversen Family. Note the spelling of "Iversen" changes to "Iverson" sometime after their arrival. Courtesy of the Scandinavian Club of Hawaii.

After four months at sea, the *Beta* eventually anchored at Ma'alaea Bay on the island of Maui on February 14, 1881. To the Nordic passengers, central Maui was a foreign land. Although the laborers had been told "Hawaii was a land where the climate was like a perpetual Norwegian summer,"[63] the island's wide, flat plain was like "a Sahara in miniature, a dreary expanse of sand and shifting sandhills."[64] Upon arrival, the *Beta* passengers were offloaded at Ma'alaea Landing, where the planters divided them by lot. According to one witness, the planters lined up the newly arrived and pinned numbers on them. Then, the planters drew corresponding numbers from an urn, determining the plantations to which the Norwegians would be assigned. The witness's account compared the degrading experience to slavery:

Maui ca. 1880. Image courtesy of the author.

"THIS MONUMENT COMMEMORATES THE ARRIVAL OF THE NORWEGIAN BARQUE *BETA* WHICH DROPPED ANCHOR NEAR THIS SPOT ON FEBRUARY 18, 1881, AND OF HER SISTER SHIP *MUSCA* WHICH ARRIVED IN HONOLULU MAY 13, 1881. THEY BROUGHT MORE THAN SIX HUNDRED NORWEGIANS, SWEDES AND DANES TO WORK IN THE SUGAR CANE FIELDS AND MILLS OF THE HAWAIIAN KINGDOM. THE FIRST AND ONLY MASS MIGRATION OF SCANDINAVIANS TO THESE ISLANDS. FOR THEIR CONTRIBUTION TO THE LIFE OF THIS LAND, AS WELL AS THOSE OF THEIR COUNTRYMEN WHO PROCEEDED OR FOLLOWED, OUR MAHALO AND ALOHA."

~Inscription on plaque below

This brass plaque, placed by the Scandinavian Centennial Commission near Ma'alaea Bay on February 14, 1981, commemorates the arrival of the ship *Beta* and the first Scandinavian immigrants to Hawaii, who came to work in the sugar cane fields in February 1881. Photograph courtesy of the author, 2012.

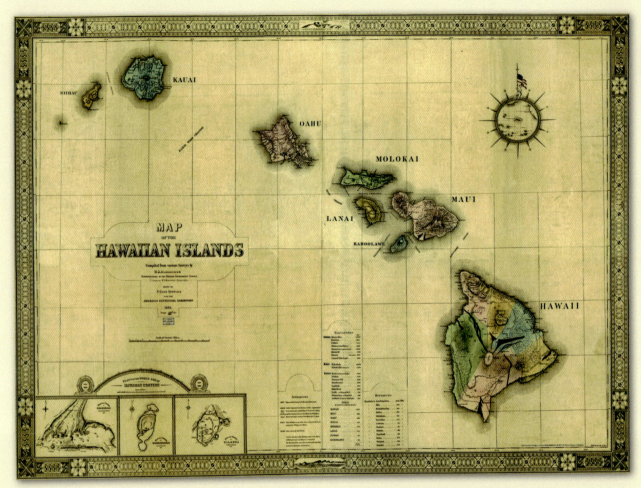

"The 1876 Centennial Map of the Kingdom." The first major map published by the Hawaiian Government Survey was prepared for the Hawaiian exhibit at the Centennial Exhibition in Philadelphia in the spring of 1876, just five year before the Scandinavians arrived at Maui in 1881. The map highlights the Islands' main topographical features, including towns, plantations, and volcanoes, for it was meant to promote the Hawaiian Kingdom to potential investors. Image courtesy of the author.

> On the 14 Februare' 1881, we arrived after much suffering, to the Sandwich Islands, to a placed called Lahaina...on the island of Maui. On board came Chr. Lorange, the slave traders' mediator....The same day we proceeded further, to a place...situated far from inhabited places. Here the trading should go on and so it did. The following day, our salesman, went ashore and returned with two natives, and six white planters. When they came on board, we were told that they were our owners....In the evening the lottery of us helpless emigrants began, and went on for a day and a night....The following day we were summoned up after nameleers [nomenclatures] and each received a thicket [sic], with different marks, applied to the breast. Some of us received no marks. These were informed that they should go to another island called Hawaii.[65]

Augusta Louise Iverson: From Norway to the Pacific Northwest

Japanese laborers (shown above), as well as those from the Azores and the Philippines, replaced Norwegian workers after the Norwegian's departure at the termination of their contracts. Spreckelsville Sugar Plantation, Maui. Painting by Joseph Dwight Strong, 1885, oil on canvas, private collection (Taito Co., Ltd., Tokyo).

The planters most likely assigned Johan Iversen to one of Castle and Cooke's three sugar plantations: Paia, Hamakuapoko, or Haiku, located in northeast Maui. Originally coming to the island as missionaries, Castle and Cooke purchased the Haiku property from King Kamehameha III and, in 1862, erected a steam-powered mill on the parcel. That year Castle and Cooke's parcels produced a 260-ton sugar crop. By 1880, the first year the company used Norwegian laborers, the parcels produced 2,600 tons of sugar.[66]

The company kept families together, so Thora and Augusta likely remained with Johan. The family lived in a house unfamiliar to Scandinavians—a single walled structure of several rooms, minus glass windows, and built of rough lumber. In addition, Maui's abundance of guavas, figs, and mangoes offended the Norwegians' bland taste buds. Admittedly, the one-time hopeful northerners found the tropical plantation experience sobering and shocking. Adding to the family's anxiety about the future, Thora gave birth to a second child, a son, Charles John, born on December 27, 1881.[67]

Augusta Louise Iverson: From Norway to the Pacific Northwest

Almost immediately, unrest and discontent appeared among the Scandinavian laborers. The strangeness of Maui's environment, coupled with contract disputes, caused the Norwegian laborers to become unhappy with their living and work conditions. Accustomed to group action and labor organization, the Scandinavians instigated one of the first labor strikes on the island, which subsequently caused an international uproar between Norway and the United States, their employers' home country. As a result, the Iversons, as well as the other Scandinavians, did not stay long, for the island kingdom was no paradise. Nor was it the promised "perpetual Norwegian summer."

Disgruntlement continued over issues such as food, flimsy housing, deductions in wages, and unfair treatment of nonworking family members by the company. Because of the problems they confronted in Hawaii, most of the Norwegian migrants left after three years when their contract expired, and they were replaced by laborers from the Azores, Japan, and the Philippines.[68]

After 1884, the Iversons disappear from the historic record until they show up in Seattle, Washington, fifteen years later.[69] Interestingly, nearly all sources—census and death records and most telling, her diary—indicated that Augusta's date of birth is October 22, but the year is often

"Maui Brand Natural Cane Sugar, Naturally Good Since 1870." Visitors can still purchase Maui sugar at the Alexander & Baldwin Sugar Mill Museum at Pauunene, Maui. Photograph courtesy of the author, 2012.

The Pioneer Square neighborhood in downtown Seattle as the Iverson family knew it at the turn of the century. From the brochure *Seattle and the Orient* (1900).

Augusta Louise Iverson:
From Norway to the Pacific Northwest

listed as "about 1884" rather than 1879. In fact, 1879 never appears in records associated with the United States. No documentation has been uncovered that explains why she would say otherwise. Perhaps Thora changed her daughter's birth date to cover up her illegitimacy. Or perhaps to match the year she entered the United States. No naturalization records have been found for Augusta, and in 1880, when she traveled with her family to Hawaii as an infant, the Sandwich Islands were governed as a kingdom—Hawaii was not annexed by the United States until 1898. Until immigration or naturalization papers for Augusta are found, if they indeed exist, the likelihood of determining the reason remains slim.

Further mysteries also remain. It is unclear when the family left Maui and when and where Johan Alfred left the family, and presumably passed away. Perhaps he returned to Norway to raise money so that his family could follow. Or, he intended to return to them somewhere in the Pacific, but became sick or died. Whatever the scenario, John Alfred disappeared sometime before 1900 and his family never returned to the Old Country. After their experience in Hawaii, it is likely the family looked to a much closer destination than Norway, one that was actively encouraging the settlement of Scandinavian immigrants—the Pacific Northwest. As early as 1876, the Scandinavian Immigration and Aid Society had formed in Seattle, with the purpose of bringing Scandinavians to the Puget Sound city. Over 12 percent of the Seattle population in 1900 was from Scandinavia or were children of Scandinavians. About half were women, a majority of whom were classified as single.[70]

It is in the Scandinavian hub of Seattle where the historic record picked up the Iverson's trail.[71] The Polk Directory listed both Augusta L. Iverson and her brother, Charles J. Iverson, in 1899. Augusta, who was twenty at the time,[72] was living at a boarding house on Lenora Street in downtown Seattle. Charles, who was eighteen, was living on First Avenue and attending the Acme Business College, whose progressive motto in 1899—"Learn to do by doing"—perfectly reflected the times.[73] The college, located on the corner of Second and Pike, initially taught shorthand and typing, but expanded its curriculum to include bookkeeping, accounting, business law, English, and mathematics.[74]

"Acme Business College" Advertised in *Polk's Seattle Directory* in 1900. (The Iverson family is listed on the same page.)

A year later it was Augusta's turn to attend school. In 1900, she was enrolled at the college, while Charles, living at an address on Second Avenue, worked as a fireman at a planing mill in north Seattle. Their mother, Thora, described as a "widow" in 1910, lived at the same downtown address as Charles.[75]

Augusta Louise Iverson: From Norway to the Pacific Northwest

In 1900, the U.S. Census recorded a "nineteen-year-old" Augusta Iverson working as a nurse for the Trimble family on Aloha Street on Lower Queen Anne Hill in Seattle.[76] The census, however, stated that this young woman came from Minnesota and described her as "Swedish," and not Norwegian. Moreover, the family's nurse would have likely been living at the family's residence, rather than living in a boarding house downtown. Still, Queen Anne Hill is not far from Lenora Street, a destination she could have accessed fairly easily using Seattle's street car system.[77] The Trimbles may have had little knowledge of Augusta's family history and thus incorrectly assumed her ethnicity and migration. Moreover, Augusta may have only worked at the Trimble household for a short time before the census was counted. Although most young single Scandinavian women worked as domestic servants in Seattle at this time, it is unclear if, in fact, the same Augusta Iverson, who eventually traveled to Alaska and married Martin Radovan, worked as a nurse for a family on the aptly named Aloha Street in 1900.

Thora Iverson's Seattle house, 1937. The Office of the Secretary of State, Division of Archives and Records Management, Puget Sound Regional Branch, Bellevue, Washington.

The search for Augusta's story has numerous twists, unknowns, and dead ends. If Augusta was in fact this family's nurse, then she figured out a way to move beyond domestic servitude rather quickly. By the time she reached Seattle, Augusta had broken ties with the country of her parents and had learned the basics of modern American life. She spoke English and, being single, she understood what tools she needed in order to support herself. While attending school, she obtained bookkeeping, typing, and accounting skills. Such expertise was advantageous in a city where numerous jobs were opening to Scandinavians. Augusta's aspirations for a better future reflected both her native country's value in education, while at the same time, her new country's belief in independence and self-reliance.[78] Ten years later, Augusta, now entering her thirties, found employment as a bookkeeper at a local Seattle office. She lived with her mother in the southwest part of Seattle in a house on which Thora was paying a mortgage.[79] Thora made ends meet as a cook.[80]

Augusta Louise Iverson:
From Norway to the Pacific Northwest

There is no way of knowing why Augusta went to Alaska. Perhaps Augusta attended the Alaska-Yukon-Pacific Exposition sometime in August 1909, attracted by the promotion of "Norway Day" or "Acme Business College Day," her alma mater.[81] Maybe Seattle's nearly five-month-long celebration of Alaska triggered an interest in the North, but if Augusta had simply read the newspaper, Alaska would have been on her mind.

Alaska and the development of its resources were central to the city's growing economy, but it also had become a focus of politics during the Roosevelt and Taft administrations. Seattle's own Richard A. Ballinger made headlines between 1906 and 1909, first as the Commissioner of the Central Land Office and then as the Secretary of the Interior, in his public battle with Louis Glavis and Chief Forester Gifford Pinchot over coal leases in Alaska.[82]

Underlying the public affair was Gifford Pinchot's fear of a Morgan-Guggenheim monopoly of Alaska's coal, which the Syndicate intended to use to fuel the CR & NW Railway and proposed coastal smelters in Cordova for Kennecott's copper. But because the federally controlled coal leases remained withdrawn and unavailable, the CR& NW Railway shifted to the more expensive oil to fuel its locomotives.[83] The unavailable coal leases, coupled with a lack of known copper reserves beyond Kennecott, led the Syndicate to reason that its plans to develop smelters in Alaska were fiscally unrealistic. To the chagrin of Cordova's businessmen, the Syndicate shelved the plans. Instead, it sought a more economically sound plan to process Kennecott's high-grade copper at smelters already established outside of Alaska, namely, in Tacoma, Washington.

The Alaska Syndicate bought the Alaska Steamship Company in 1909 to support construction of the CR & NW Railway, supply the mill and mines, and transport copper ore mined in the Wrangell Mountains to the Guggenheims' smelters just south of Seattle, in Tacoma.[84] They merged the Alaska Steamship Company with the Northwestern Steamship Company, keeping the Alaska Steamship Company name. Ironically, the merger of the two companies gave Morgan and the Guggenheims a near monopoly of the Alaska shipping industry. The transaction occurred in 1908, and was perhaps overshadowed in Seattle by the golden-hyped A-Y-P Exposition. Nevertheless, the shipping deal, which effectively solved Kennecott's transportation problems, allowed the Syndicate to focus on developing the mill and mines, an operation that eventually earned investors $100 million in profit and quickly became the Nizina district's primary economic engine.

This Alaskan venture with direct ties to the Northwest undoubtedly affected the lives of Augusta and Martin, too. At the very least, for someone with Augusta's skills, Alaska meant employment. Indeed, that was the case for Martin, whose interest in railroad construction initially brought him north.[85] In all likelihood, both individuals found their way to Alaska aboard an Alaska Steamship Company ship.

Although Augusta and Martin both lived in Seattle for a time, as far as we know, their paths never crossed. They were two Europeans—one with roots in the north, the other the south—who emigrated from their native lands, taking entirely different routes. One came to America alone, following a common pattern familiar to many

The Alaska Yukon Pacific Exposition (A-Y-P) took place in Seattle, at the University of Washington campus, in 1909. Organized to commemorate the Alaska gold rush, the World's Fair drew more than three million visitors. The A-Y-P Exposition not only revitalized interest in the North, but served as a public relations opportunity for women, as emphasized by the Fair's official logo. The circular seal displayed three women from their respective regions: the Orient, Alaska, and Canada, each holding the keys to wealth: an Ocean Steamer, Gold, and a Railway Locomotive.

Augusta Louise Iverson:
From Norway to the Pacific Northwest

The National Creek building was the first structure constructed at Kennecott and was also the office where Augusta worked. Photograph by the author, National Park Service, 2010.

immigrants, and initially entered the United States on the East Coast. The other was brought to America by her family who had traveled to an exotic Pacific island and eventually entered on the West Coast. Both found their way to the Pacific Northwest. At the time, Seattle, the hailed gateway to Alaska, directly linked the Northwest to the copper mines at Kennecott. Each person journeyed north, driven by their individual needs and dreams. Only after arriving in Alaska did Martin and Augusta find each other, deep in the heart of the Wrangell Mountains.

Gold, Copper and Love:
Life in Early Blackburn and McCarthy
1912–1919

It was rumors of gold that first brought prospectors to the Wrangell Mountains, but it was copper that kept them there.

~ United States Geological Survey (USGS)[86]

After four years of railway work, Martin Radovan remained in the Nizina Mining District, taking whatever job was available. USGS had recognized the Nizina district in 1908 after a favorable reconnaissance survey of the so-called "copper belt" located just south of the Wrangell Mountains. Named for the Nizina River, a northern branch of the Chitina River, the new district afforded USGS geologists the opportunity to solve the region's geologic puzzle; to provide support for the placer mining that had been conducted in the area since 1901; and to observe and mine valuable copper ore.[87]

In 1912, Martin took his first mining job in the Nizina district at Chititu Creek with a hydraulic mining company called the Andrus Mining Company. That first year, Martin placer-mined for Andrus through the summer months; by winter, he had built a cabin in a ravine below Nikolai Butte on Dan Creek, a tributary of the Nizina River. The cabin was situated near Boulder Creek, on a bluff overlooking Dan Creek. From his cabin, Martin viewed sheep grazing on Williams Peak to the south, the creekside gold camp to the west, and the Copper Creek drainage to the east. Using his cabin as a base, the thirty-one-year-old began prospecting throughout the Nizina River watershed, including Young, Dan and Glacier creeks.[88]

Six years prior, in 1906, a prospector named John Barrett had found a vein of chalcocite on top of a cliff along McCarthy Creek. The chalcocite was 70 percent pure copper, the same quality as the Bonanza

ABOVE: Early McCarthy, date unknown. Courtesy of Jim Edwards.

"Dan Creek Miners Bring in Big Pokes of Gold Dust." *The Chitina Leader*, January 21, 1911.

deposit, located in the contact a few miles away. Barrett had good foresight to recognize that the only economical way to access the copper prospects located thousands of feet above the Kennicott Glacier was by railroad. Most significantly, any railroad built to access the copper ore would have to cross land bordered by the Kennicott Glacier and McCarthy Creek.[89]

In July of 1906, one year before the Alaska Syndicate began to mark locations for the CR & NW Railway line, Barrett decided to stake a homestead of 296 acres at the mouth of McCarthy Creek. Because Barrett had staked the most desirable land in the McCarthy Creek area, the company ended up renting part of Barrett's homestead for a freight yard.[90] By 1911, Kennecott had built a bunkhouse, cookhouse, depot, and water tower on Barrett's property.[91] Concerned that renting too much of his homestead before the title process was complete might invite legal problems, Barrett began to discourage newcomers, attracted to the budding, but closed, company town of Kennecott, from tenting on his land. But with completion of the railroad, businessmen and merchants continued to arrive along with prospectors and miners. The new arrivals began to congregate just north of Barrett's homestead.

Gold, Copper, and Love:
Life in Early Blackburn and McCarthy

They called the booming community Blackburn.

Blackburn started at the site of another homestead near the railroad, belonging to John Blomquist, who also staked his claims in 1906. The first businessmen in the area were the Fagerburg brothers, who ran a small store at the mining camp at Nizina. In 1911, the Fagerburg brothers constructed the Blackburn Roadhouse, a two-story structure built with logs and milled wood. At the time, it was considered the "biggest log structure in the district."[92] The Fagerburgs' roadhouse played a key role in the first ascent of Mount Blackburn, the tallest peak in the Wrangell Mountains.[93] In early August of 1911, mountaineer Dora Keen outfitted at Fagerburgs' roadhouse and hired John Barrett and three other experienced men to serve as packers and helpers. Keen was not successful in her first attempt, but she returned in the spring of 1912 and made it to the top of Mount Blackburn.[94]

R.F. McClellan, superintendent at Kennecott Mine, organized Keen's first expedition and had secured local prospectors to complete her outfit. Apparently, a young Martin Radovan assisted with the 1911 expedition, supplying logistical support.[95] He was not named in the party that made the failed ascent, however, and it is unclear how Martin actually participated in the expedition. Keen, in an article for *Scribner's Magazine*, noted that numerous prospectors served as "guides" and members of a "relief party." She also made the point that "my men had been...Americans all, Mr. McClellan knew them....He wanted men 'whom he could count on to put a hundred pounds on their backs and go where he told them,' and he had found them, not far from the Road House."[96] Although he can be placed in the area at that time, clearly knew the terrain, and could easily pack a hundred pounds, Martin, who spoke with a thick Slavic accent, was not an American, and Keen may have overlooked or ignored his efforts in her account of the climb. Nevertheless, whether his role was minor or more involved, Martin Radovan, according to sources close to him, participated in the historic event.

In 1912, the same year as Keen's successful ascent, the townsite of Blackburn was laid out on a slit of land between Barrett's and Blomquist's homesteads, and, not surprisingly, a construction boom quickly followed. That same year, Oscar Breedman, a hotel owner with ties to Chitina and Cordova, bought the Fagerburgs' hotel. John Blomquist, the new mayor of Blackburn, predicted to a Valdez paper that a great future lay ahead for the new interior town.[97] Convinced that there was money to be made, Martin Radovan took a job running the restaurant at the Blackburn Roadhouse in 1913. Running the restaurant with him was "one of Kennecott's secretaries," Augusta Iverson.[98]

Martin and Augusta's flirtation in the restaurant business was brief due primarily to Blackburn's sudden economic downturn caused by the Shushanna gold rush.[99] In July 1913, miners discovered gold in the Shushanna country, about eighty miles from Blackburn on the north side of the Wrangell Mountains. The

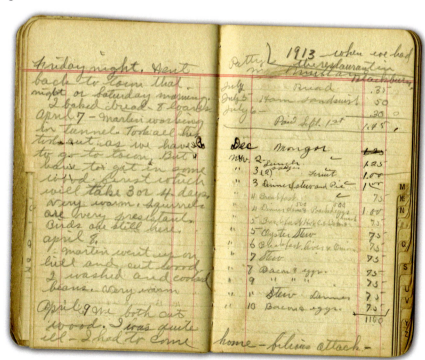

Augusta reused an old ledger from 1913 for her daily journal entries in 1930. A scribble "1913 when we had the restaurant in Blackburn" explains the reason for the faded list of meals and prices, apparently written seventeen years prior. From Augusta Radovan's Journal. Martin Radovan Private Collection.

Gold, Copper, and Love:
Life in Early Blackburn and McCarthy

The Blackburn Roadhouse, circa 1911. Courtesy of Jim Edwards.

discovery ignited the last major gold rush in Alaska, which subsequently depopulated the Nizina watershed, including the fledgling towns and camps of McCarthy, Blackburn, Chitina, Dan Creek, and Chititu. However, the surging number of miners and merchants arriving each day on the railway inundated Barrett's homestead with squatters. It is unknown if Martin went to Shushanna, but as proprietor of the roadhouse, he was a firsthand witness to the rush.

James Edwards, a long-time McCarthy resident and friend of Martin, recalls that "Radovan advertised his roadhouse as offering a meal and guide service. The meal: a bowl of beans. The guide service: 'Shushanna is that-a-way.'"[100] Meanwhile, Barrett, in order to accommodate the influx of newcomers, incorporated the town of McCarthy.[101] Undoubtedly, the need for grubstakes and outfits for Shushanna sparked the development of McCarthy's commercial infrastructure, but the stampede that took miners over the Wrangell Mountains and out of the Nizina country had a dire effect on Blackburn. Because the railroad stopped at McCarthy and not Blackburn, most passengers stayed in McCarthy and made nearly all their purchases from McCarthy's merchants. Consequently, the one-time promising town of Blackburn began to shrivel."[102] Martin and Augusta, therefore, ran the roadhouse for, at most, two more years.

In spite of Blackburn's inevitable decline, Martin and Augusta remained involved with the community well into the 1920s and early 1930s. The couple was married by the Justice of the Peace in McCarthy on February 27, 1914,[103] and spent their honeymoon at the Blackburn Roadhouse.[104] When and where the couple met remains a mystery, but Martin briefly worked at Kennecott, at the same time as Augusta. Between December 1916 and January 1917, Martin paid a deduction for "All Married Men at Kennecott."[105] Martin listed himself as an "unemployed machinist" on his World War I draft card, implying that he worked for an employer, in this case, Kennecott.[106] Martin had a homestead near McCarthy, and on several occasions in her diary Augusta makes reference to a place they resided at while in "town." "Town" was undoubedly McCarthy, but according to Martin, he did not make improvements on the McCarthy homestead and eventually "lost the land."[107]

Gold, Copper, and Love:
Life in Early Blackburn and McCarthy

It is also unclear as to where exactly the couple was living in 1914, but they had ties to the port town of Cordova, Alaska. In 1918, Martin listed Cordova as his permanent residence and named "Mrs. Augusta Louise Radovan of Cordova, Alaska" his nearest relative.[108] In 1924, Augusta was called to Cordova for jury duty, becoming one of Alaska's first generation of female voters to do so. She served for several weeks, returning to McCarthy on November 8. The call to public service also offered another clue as to the couple's tie to the coastal town.[109] Unfortunately, any of the associated records of the Radovan's early life in Cordova likely burned in one of the many fires that swept through town in the 1940s, 1950s, and 1960s.[110]

One important record that survived was the Radovans' marriage certificate. Present at the couple's wedding on that February day were two witnesses: Frank A. Iverson and Anna Sornes.[111] Although they shared a last name, Frank Iverson was not related to Augusta. He was originally from the Dakotas, and, like Martin, made his way to Alaska via Seattle. Frank worked as a surveyor in the Puget Sound city at approximately the same time Augusta's family lived there, but it is unknown if the families knew each other then.[112] As with Martin, Frank Iverson came to Alaska to work on the CR & NW Railway. He lived in Chitina between 1911 and 1912, and then sometime after that, he homesteaded near Blackburn. Frank Iverson operated the McCarthy Dairy during the 1920s and was one of about five local farmers who supplied vegetables and other agricultural products to Kennecott.[113] He was married to Anna Sornes by 1920. Anna was born in Norway, immigrated in 1912, and was similar in age to Augusta.[114] Considering Anna witnessed Augusta's nuptials, it can be assumed the women, who shared a common background and story, were good friends.

Martin Radovan and Augusta Iverson were married in McCarthy on February 27, 1914. The newlyweds spent their honeymoon at the Blackburn Roadhouse. The State of Alaska Bureau of Vital Statistics.

Besides being friendly, the couples shared life experiences shaped by broad historic patterns and trends. Unlike Augusta Iverson's family, Frank Iverson followed a traditional immigration route for Scandinavians: His family first migrated to the Midwest, then to the Pacific Northwest, then to Alaska.[115] Although it is unclear how Anna ended up in McCarthy, it is important to note that she came to work for Kennecott as a single person, and, like Augusta, presumably met her husband after she had arrived. In addition, both women—whether it was farming or mining—worked side by side with their husbands. These actions not only reflect traditional roles of Scandinavian wives, but they hint at a pattern where, instead of women following men north (known as "reluctant pioneers"), women like Anna and Augusta came to Kennecott for their own reasons and were hired on their own merits, and only afterwards chose to get married. In other words, these women were anything but passive players in history: They played active roles in their work, marriages, and communities, and their desire for coming to Alaska in the first place was their own, too.[116]

Five years before the Radovans were married by McCarthy's Justice of the Peace, the United States Congress established four judicial districts to cover the Territory of Alaska. The Third District covered Cordova, Valdez, Chitina, Kennicott, and McCarthy.[117] Except for mining claims and his marriage, Martin's only other known legal dealing was a supposed felony. On March 9, 1914, *The Alaska Citizen* reported that Martin Radovan was indicted for

Sourdough Tells Of Early Days In Territory

Saturday, November 4, 1972 Anchorage Daily Times—3A

(Continued from Page 2) ping business that handled grapes and wine, and made himself a millionaire, not knowing that his brother was alive in the wilds of Alaska.

Meanwhile both Radovan's sisters died and it was until 1966 that the brothers found each other.

In Cordova in 1965, Radovan met a fisherman that spent his winters in Delano. He happened to mention that he had a brother in Delano, and the fisherman recognized the name.

The fisherman returned to Delano and related the news to his brother Radovich.

In the late fall of 1966 Radovich flew to Cordova to find his brother. He chartered a plane and it took two days for him to find Radovan, who was in the middle of moving from his summer prospecting to his winter cabin.

"Radovich talked to me a while, not letting me know who he was," said Radovan. "He asked me some questions, and then asked me if I had a brother. I told him I did, and that my brother's name was Jack. He put his hands on his hips and said, 'I'm Jack'."

Radovich wanted his Sourdough brother to go to Delano immediately with him, but Radovan had some good claims and he was preparing for the winter.

"I can't go, I have to lay in my winter supplies and lay out feed for the birds," Radovan told him.

"To hell with that," said Radovich.

"To hell with you," said Radovan.

Radovan finally agreed to go after his supplies were taken care of and he had spent time in Delano meeting his brother's family.

Radovan returned to Alaska and his claims turned out to be quite valuable. Radovan says that the U.S. Bureau of Mines sent geologists to his property and that in its Virginia offices the bureau has it recorded that his claim has 4.5 million tons of the richest copper bearing ore in the United States. It's some of the same ore that made the Kennicott strike big.

In 1968, Radovan says he sold exploratory rights to the claims to a friend who had the finances to back the exploration. Radovan received a $20,000 check, and was to receive installments on the rest of the payment every year until the rights expired, on June 1, 1974.

However, the rights were soon sold to a Mr. Thomas of Tampa, Fla., who hoped to back the development of the claim. In 1969 Thomas in turn sold the rights to the Geneva-Pacific Corporation of Illinois.

In 1969, Radovan spent the winter in Cordova, the first time he had left the claim for any length of time. When he returned the next spring he found all of his firewood had been burned, his cookshack was pushed off into a creek, and the company had set up its own camp.

"Since those guys set up camp all the animals have left the gulch," said Radovan. "There are shotgun shells all over the creek. My birds were tame, they went to them like they came to me, and last year they were killed."

"We only killed what we needed to eat here, or like the bear, where it was the only cure," said Radovan. "Now some people can get up there in a car and they kill everything they see."

"Copper is scarce and my strike is rich, but I don't have the money to stop them," he said.

Radovan plans to let the lease run out, and then try to have the government mine the copper.

Meanwhile, Radovan is leaving Alaska to go to Delano where the rest of his family is.

"They're so convincing down there for me to stay," said Radovan. "I don't have to do anything there, and I travel all over with my brother."

"I stopped in Anchorage to have my will made up, so I can leave my money to the poor," said Radovan.

Asked if he would ever return to Cordova, Radovan smiled and said, "Oh, maybe, I don't know. I like to help the kids there."

"All the kids like me in Cordova," he smiled.

> "Radovich talked to me for a while, not letting me know who he was. He asked me some questions, and then he asked me if I had a brother. I told him I did."

THERE WERE NO TV DINNERS IN 1915
Radovans wife, Augusta, not only had to cook dinner on early camping trips, she had to catch it. This picture was taken on a camping trip a few years after they were married, probably on an expedition to fill the meat larder.

A photograph of Augusta Radovan from 1915 appeared in an article about the pioneering life of Martin Radovan. *Anchorage Daily Times*, November 4, 1972.

---

alleged robbery at McCarthy, but was "granted his freedom by order of Judge Brown" because the district attorney was unable to locate witnesses, and "there was not available evidence to insure [sic] conviction."[118] The only other altercation described in association with Martin was a story told by James Edwards. "While Martin was in charge of the Blackburn roadhouse," recalled Edwards, "a patron once ran off without paying, and Martin Radovan chased him down and got his money."[119] There is no way of knowing if the incidents were related, or even what the circumstances were surrounding them.[120] But they do suggest that Martin was no "pushover." He was as tough as the town's reputation and, like many of McCarthy's inhabitants, took the law into his own hands when he believed it necessary to do so.

As the boomtown of Blackburn declined, Augusta was also doing what was necessary to support their chosen lifeway. She returned to Kennecott in 1918 to work as a bookkeeper in the milltown's first building, constructed at a site near National Creek. Due to skyrocketing copper prices sparked by World War I, Kennecott had enjoyed record profits for the previous four years.[121] In addition, rich new finds of ore were discovered in the Jumbo and the Mother Lode mines. High copper prices encouraged the mines and mill to operate around the clock, creating a need for more labor. This probably attracted Augusta's younger brother, Charles John Iverson, to Kennecott. By 1918, Charlie, or C.J., as he was also called, was working at the mill as a receiving clerk.[122] He worked for Kennecott at least two more years.[123] Charles returned to Washington state by the end of the decade, presumably to take care of the siblings' aging mother, Thora Iverson.[124] Augusta also left the mill town, for the U.S. census in 1920 found the Radovans living at Martin's cabin at Dan Creek.[125]

Charles John Iverson listed his mother's residence in Seattle as his permanent address on his World War I draft registration card. He also revealed that he worked as a receiving clerk for the Kennecott Copper Corporation in Alaska. A job he likely received because his sister, Augusta, worked there too.

Martin and Augusta at Dan Creek
1920–1931

And now let us consider what manner of women we shall endeavor to be, to the end that the world may find in us the inspiration of which it is so sorely in need.

~Margaret Harrais,
McCarthy resident, WCTU Vice President, and Augusta's friend
"A Prayer for All Women"[126]

I went down to bridge to see Martin. Had lunch there. Martin works at night on boiler. Very lovely day. Good walking. Got home very tired.

~Augusta Radovan
Journal entry, April 14, 1930

In 1920 Martin listed his occupation as "placer miner." Though he had a tendency to provide false information to census takers, this statement was undoubtedly true. For Martin—with constant help from Augusta—spent nearly every day digging his mountainside tunnel or sluicing at creekside for gold.

Miners at Dan Creek employed, as their main mining method, a hydraulic system. A strong spray of water loosened and transported gold-bearing gravels to the sluice boxes for recovery of the gold. The system enabled miners to move huge mounds of dirt in order to expose older placer gold deposits.[127] The growth of the depot town of McCarthy brought road and communication connections with the booming gold-mining camps. The Nizina road was the longest in the district. It crossed the Nizina River by a long bridge two miles west of

ABOVE: Martin prospected for both placer and lode gold at his camp on upper Dan Creek, date unknown. Martin Radovan Private Collection.

The McCARTHY Weekly News

VOL. 5.   McCARTHY, ALASKA, SATURDAY October 21st, 1922.   No. 50.

ELECTION NOVEMBER 7

So that the voters of this section can become familiar with the candidates at the general election, November 7th., we are publishing the tickets on page 2.

Dan Sutherland for delegate, will undoubtely come romping home.

The choice for Senator lies between Thos. Wade of Anchorage and Anthony J. Dimond of Valdez. This section will go strong for Toney but Wade has a following to the westward that will be hard to overcome.

For Representatives there are six candidates, only four to be elected. The Republican party has a strong ticket in the field but Tom Price, on the democratic ticket, is going to give his opponents a run for their money, in fact it is a foregone conclusion that he will be elected. E E. Ray, of Cordova, is also a fac in the race which is not overlooked by the Republican party.

The Division, however, will be well represented at Juneau next Spring as all the candidates are thoroughly familiar with the conditions and the needs of the territory.

At this election the women of the territory will take a very active part, it depending on their vote alone, whether they will serve as Jurors at $5.00 per diem. We do not think this amendment will pass as it is a certainty that the average Alaskan woman would prefer to remain at home, looking after her children, than to be summoned to court to act as Juror in some disreputable case which under

MINING NEWS

Warren Nelson, who arrived in town on Thursday, brings some very encouraging reports from the Dan Creek section, He has been prospecting on Copper Creek for the past year and is confident that some day it will be a producer.

On the Jack Pot group, Dexter Coyouette has a surface show of pay ovea 800 feet long.

This property is owned by his brother Clifford, and joins Nelson's property on the East

Martin Rodavan and wife, who are prospecting benches on the right limit of Dan Creek have found the old Klofer and Meyers pay streak which produced such rich clean-ups five years ago. This pay was known to exist but hard to locate since it had been cut off by a gulch.

The pay is about fifty feet in width and pans running from five to thirteen dollars are obtained,

The Rodavans have worked hard on this property and deserve all the good luck that will now come their way.

Bob Johnson and Charley Range will be in charge of the Dan Creek Mining Company's property this winter.

JUST RECEIVED,

A fresh shipment of Beef, Pork Mutton, Veal, Sausage, Head Cheese, Fresh Ranch Eggs, and Jersey Butter.
Your Patronage solicited.

TELEGRAPHIC

Vladavosteck, Oct. 19. Special to Weekly News. American and British Marines were landed here today to guard the respective offices of the Consulate.

Constantinoble, Oct. 19. Moscow protested today to Fngland against the removal of the Soviet Government flag from the Russian legation here.

London, Oct. 19. After an important conference with King George, Bonar Law began the formation of a new cabinet, in succession to the Lloyd George government.

Seattle, Oct. 20. The Alaska Steamship Co. today awarded the Todd shipyard at Tacoma, the contract for the construction of a twin screw 16 knot steel passenger and freight liner for the Alaskan service.

A shipment of hay from Fred Overlander's ranche at Long Lake was sold to local parties.

Mr. and Mrs. R. E. Lander, of Anchorage, are recent arrivals in our city. Mr. Lander is at present employed by the Mother Lode Coalition Co, but owing to the shortage of houses at Kennecott he will secure a residence in McCarthy.

John Nickell returned to town yesterday, after a successfull hunting trip in Skolai Basin section.

George Anderson made a good buy this week—purchasing a garden rake, and a pastry roller for Emil, for two bits.

After 21 months' service in the Power Plant at Kennecott, W Godfry will spend the next ten

LOCAL NEWS

REAL ESTATE DEALS

Frank Iverson has purchased the Lubbe barn and lot from Mrs. Elizabeth Lubbé.

Mr. Iverson will practically rebuild this barn, making it more suitable for his business, the surplus lumber and iron roofing will be used to improve his buibdings on the farm across the river,

John Amber has disposed of two of his residences to Mr. Trim. The property is located next to the Pioneer Hall. Mrs. Trim will be down very shortly from the wood camp to make her home in McCarthy, as the eldest child is now of school age.

Pending the construction of a permanent bridge by the A, R. C. across the Kennecott, Messrs. Anderson and Iverson have commenced the building ef a temporary bridge, in order to haul supplies to and from their farms.

Emil Isaacson has completed his Fall plouging.
Olaf Holtet secured the contract for hauling the U.S, Marshal's coal.

FARMER LOSES CROP

'Red Whiskers' is no more, a joker foolishly betting Bill Henry, a prominent stock raiser in this section, a brand new hat that he would not dare to take a chance on Bill Longley cutting his crop off. Bill is wearing the hat and looks like a two year old

"Mining News Report." *The McCarthy Weekly News*, October 21, 1922.

Martin and Augusta at Dan Creek

Upper Reaches of Dan Creek, date unknown. Martin Radovan Private Collection.

the mouth of Young Creek. At the roadhouse on May Creek, one mile east of Young Creek, the road forked, one branch going to Dan Creek and the other to Chititu Creek. Labor and materials were easily imported into these areas, leading to more aggressive hydraulic mining at Dan Creek. Stephen Birch had been involved in Dan Creek mining since 1901 and had invested in an extensive hydraulic system by 1918. While Birch served as president of the newly formed Kennecott Copper Company,[128] his brother ran the placer mine.

John J. Price and Lewis A. Levensaler obtained Birch's Dan Creek property, forming the Nicolai Placer Mines Company in 1927.[129] A crew of fourteen men worked for Price. Earl Pilgrim, Inspector for Alaska's Territorial Department of Mines, reported that "the discovery...of additional bench deposits...justify[s] the belief that profitable placer operations will continue on Dan Creek for many years."[130] Besides hydraulic mining, miners also attempted lode mining along the creek. By 1931, a 200-foot tunnel was driven to develop the hard-rock deposit on a property held by John Barrett, situated on Williams Peak opposite the mouth of Dan Creek, near the site of Martin's cabin.[131]

Meanwhile, Martin began to work a number of placer and lode claims on upper Dan Creek not far from his cabin. He named the placer claims Bessie Nos. 1 & 2, while the lode claims were called Augusta 1-8.[132] The on-going economic boom re-populated the Dan Creek area, which began to serve as a kind of suburb of McCarthy. It is probably safe to say that Augusta enjoyed the Dan Creek location for its proximity to town and its subsequent social life. By the 1920s, the couple had become well-known and seemingly respected by their fellow residents. When good fortune descended upon them, the town rejoiced. The *McCarthy Weekly News* heralded in 1922 that Martin and Augusta found the "old Klofer and Meyers pay streak" near a hard-to-locate area in a gulch. The paper added that "The Rodavans [sic] have worked hard on this property and deserve all the good luck that will come their way."[133]

Augusta made her way to town far more often then Martin. Martin usually went to McCarthy for reasons such as a broken finger[134] or to pass through on his way to Valdez or Cordova for mining business.[135] If he did go to McCarthy, Martin never stayed long.[136] Augusta, on the other hand, was observed Christmas shopping in "the big city."[137] She often accompanied Mrs. and Mr. John J. Price, who, in addition to operating his mining company, served as Dan Creek's postmaster from May 1924 until mail service was discontinued in April 1932.[138] Augusta, who had postal work experience herself, was likely assisting Price with his postal duties.[139] McCarthyites admired the Radovans. The *McCarthy Weekly News* reported on March 28, 1925, that "Mr. and Mrs. Martin Radovan walked in from Dan Creek this week. They say they could have ridden in but, like the retreating soldier, they didn't want any horse to hold them back."[140]

Martin and Augusta at Dan Creek

Martin drew an "X" along the ridgeline, marking what he called the "Dan Creek Prospect." Martin Radovan Private Collection.

Insightful information about Martin and Augusta's marriage and life at Dan Creek is scattered throughout the historic record. She is mentioned only incidentally in newspaper interviews conducted with Martin as well as in other popular accounts about his life. The most informative source about the couple is a diary Augusta kept between April 1930 and June 1931. Characteristically practical, Augusta wrote her daily thoughts in an old business ledger that had originally been intended as a way to keep track of customers running tabs at the Blackburn Roadhouse restaurant in 1913. For example, under "I" it lists a tab for Frank Iverson, who ate numerous meals at the roadhouse from November 17 to December 25, 1913 including "two Thanksgiving Turkey Dinners for $3.00" and an "eleven-and-a- half-pound ham for $3.22."[141] Seventeen years later, she recycled the ledger, filling its blank pages with daily accounts of her life with Martin at Dan Creek.

Absent from the journal are any romantic discussions about Martin or their marriage. On their wedding anniversary, for example, she wrote, "Martin went down and got our stuff. Lou and Ole ran into rim at end of 50ft tunnel. We carried everything up hill." Then, almost as an afterthought, she added, "Feb 27. Our wedding anniversary." Nevertheless, her journal clearly describes two people who were content and committed, and who shared a common goal. She visited him regularly at work, usually bringing him lunch. She never complained about his devotion to mining, and even when it was clear that cabin life was rather lonely and monotonous, Augusta put on a stoic face. One Easter Sunday she lamented, "Sun shining and no Easter bonnet to wear." But then she reasoned, "Would have no place to wear it if I had one. So it's alright."[142]

The couple also shared a common interest in the comings and goings of the local wildlife. Augusta wrote prolifically about the animals that visited them at Dan Creek. On April 13, 1930, she "counted six sheep" on the mountain behind the cabin. On January 16, she counted eight little birds, one woodpecker, fifteen magpies, and one weasel. Throughout the spring, Augusta kept her eye on a curious coyote, dreamed of bears, and on May 28, 1931, she observed a big porcupine outside her cabin door. "Its lots of fun watching him through the window," she wrote, "I put out some dried apples for him but he didn't take any."[143] Interacting with the local wildlife brought pleasure to Augusta, and apparently to the animals as well. "Fed the birds," wrote Augusta on returning to Dan Creek after a week's absence, "They were glad to see us back." Martin also cared deeply for the animals. Years later he had told a reporter for the *Anchorage Daily Times* that, while working on the railway, he had made friends with numerous black bears and "had one eating out of my hand within three days."[144]

Martin and Augusta at Dan Creek

Had it been a different time Martin and Augusta, with their keen eyesight and interest in observing animals, could have been wildlife biologists. But repeated habituation, feeding, and anthropomorphizing of the surrounding wildlife suggests that, perhaps, it was more than a hobby. Augusta and Martin never had children, yet there was something "parental" in their relationship with nature. On May 29, 1931, for example, Augusta walked down to the lower camp and along the way noticed a mother bird feeding her chick. "One of them tucks a piece of bread into the mouth of another," she described endearingly. "It must have been a baby."[145] At first glance the Radovans' rapport with the local wildlife seems trivial. But the relationship clearly pleased Augusta, who spent countless hours alone at the cabin. Moreover, the wildlife was significant to Martin, especially later in life, for the animals he befriended provided him with a sense of happiness and companionship, not unlike children who bring comfort to their aging parents.

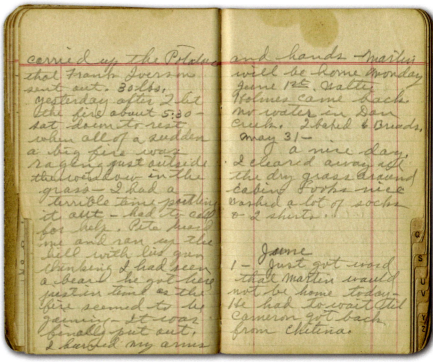
Augusta's journal entry for May 30, 1930 describes a grass fire near the Dan Creek cabin. Putting out fires was one of many tasks that Augusta endured at camp while Martin tunneled. Martin Radovan Private Collection.

Martin's mining endeavors at Dan Creek meant that the couple's daily routines were spent apart. Cabin life required they take on different tasks and responsibilities. Augusta's journal provides daily testimony of Martin's persistent and somewhat obsessed mining activities. In their search for gold, the pair maintained at least two Dan Creek camps: a lower camp at creekside at which they sluiced for gold, and an upper camp in which Martin tunneled into the mountainside in search of ancient bedrock. On February 18, 1931, Augusta wrote, "Martin went to work in tunnel." On March 1, he "reached the rim [rock] in the tunnel today. It goes up slanting a little enough to get a foot hold."[146] Two days later, she helped him "measure tunnel and height of rim." On March 10, "Martin got an early start in the tunnel," and on April 1, "Martin struck second point in tunnel," adding optimistically, "might be something there." Martin's objective at Dan Creek was clearly gold, because as Augusta noted, he "found a big piece of copper but no gold with it."[147] Also, Martin was not prospecting alone at Dan Creek. Price and "the boys" were tunneling into the rim rock just down the creek from Martin's prospects. Augusta's journal entry for March 2 reported:

> *Martin climbing rim trying to get to bed rock level. 20 above. Lou called from Creek bottom and said there was a letter for me. I went down and got it from Mrs. Kay. Price brought it up to their tunnel on Boulder Creek. They too are climbing the rim. Pretty well discouraged [by] both of these.*[148]

While Martin remained focused on his tunnel work, Augusta filled her days with a variety of household tasks. On March 19, 1931, she wrote, "I baked bread—7 loves and got wood. Martin working in tunnel. Sun is shining." Depending on the season, Augusta fished at the creek, hauled water up the hill from the creek, cut firewood, and even placer mined on her own. Cabin life could be dangerous, however. During a dry stretch in May, the grass near the cabin caught fire:

Martin and Augusta at Dan Creek

Yesterday after 2:00 lit the fire. About 5:30 sat down to rest when all of a sudden a big fire was raging just outside the window in the grass. I had a terrible time putting it out—had to call for help. Pete heard me and ran up the hill with his gun thinking I had seen a bear. He got here just in time as the fire seemed to be gaining. It was finally put out. I burned my arms and hands.

Then, without giving the fire or her injuries a second thought, she wrote, "Martin will be home Monday June 1. Walter Holmes came back. No water in Dan Creek. I baked 6 breads." The next day, without complaint of pain or dramatic discussion of the close-call, she wrote matter-of-factly: "cleared away all the dry grass around cabin."

The crisis aside, Augusta's account of cabin life was, in her mind, completely ordinary. On May 22 she wrote, "Cleaned and fixed my house. Nothing new. Cleaned and sluiced." Though life at Dan Creek appeared uneventful for both Martin and Augusta, these accounts are important because they construct a realistic portrait of miners and their mining society in the Nizina district. Contrary to popular frontier mythology, most miners and their families lived fairly ordinary lives.[149] Thus, besides providing insight into what might be assumed is the lonely and isolated life of a prospector's wife, Augusta's journal in many ways offers just the opposite. It provides a glimpse of the social life in the surrounding mining community, implying that the Radovans were part of a larger community at Dan Creek. She paints a picture of the individuals who inhabited the creekside camps, frequently mentioning the activities of Postmaster J.J. Price and Pete Eikland, who worked during the winter as a carrier on the McCarthy-Chisana mail route. She also talked often of Lou Anderton, Cliff [last name unknown], and Ole [last name unknown]—the so-called "boys," who occupied the tent camp at the bottom of the hill. Atop the hill was the Radovans' cabin, from which Augusta, like a mother hen, kept track of their whereabouts.

On March 7, 1931, Augusta wrote, "Saw Lou, Ole and Cliff coming up the creek. Cliff stayed all night with them." On March 22 she noted, "Pete just came up the creek with his dogs," and on April 3 she observed, "Saw man going down creek at 6:30. Looked like Ole."[150] From these seemingly innocuous observations emerge a situation in which people, instead of living solitary frontier existences, look out for each other. In fact, it appears that Augusta truly cared for the group of bachelors she fondly called "the boys." At times she seems protective: "Lou and Ole quit, claiming Cliff double-crossed them." She even treated them like family: "Lou and Ole came up and spent the evening," she wrote on March 13, "Lou asked me to wash and iron his shirt—I couldn't refuse—but will not charge for it. He wants to wear it to town."[151] Underpinning Augusta's motherly attention to the bachelors is the practice that, in Alaska's early mining societies, not only did people socialize together; they looked out for each other as well.[152]

The mining community that materializes from the pages of Augusta's journal exhibits, in big ways and small, the same social norms as any rural town in America. In what was generally perceived as a male-dominated frontier that supposedly lacked a social class structure, a majority of the social organizers and cultural facilitators in this Nizina community were in fact women. Unlike Martin who spent most of his time at his tunnels, part of Augusta's daily routine consisted of calling upon the wives of other miners. On May 30, 1931, Augusta wrote, "I went down and called on Mrs. Price…Mrs. Price thinks the boys don't work hard enough—she is disgusted with them." Besides the Prices, there were other mining couples with whom Augusta interacted. For example:

Went to foot of hill and Mrs. Malhorn and Mrs. Holmes were there having arrived the night before. They were in bed all tired out. The men Pete, Ole and Walter were eating their lunch. The women brought the mail from the Road H[ouse]. One letter for me from Mrs. Kay. I stopt [sic] and talked to them about 20 minutes then came home. Lots of Mosquitoes. [153]

Martin and Augusta at Dan Creek

Because the wagon road and Nizina Bridge made transportation between Dan Creek and McCarthy relatively easy, the social network extended beyond the camp and into town. During a trip to McCarthy and Blackburn, Augusta "saw Mrs. Sel[lenrers], Mrs. Barrett and Mrs. Harrais."[154] These were all women who had achieved a high level of social stature within the Nizina mining community. Mrs. Barrett's husband founded McCarthy and had a profitable lode gold operation at Williams Peak. Margaret Harrais was a leader in the Alaska chapter of the Woman's Christian Temperance Union (WCTU). Her husband, Martin Luther Harrais, had worked at Kennecott for several years.[155]

Augusta often brought Martin his lunch while he worked for the Alaska Road Commission near the Nizina Bridge site in order to earn extra money. This photo, taken in 1991 by Jet Lowe of HAER, shows all that remains of the Nizina Bridge, located at Mile 8, Nizina Road, in the McCarthy vicinity.

Like Augusta, Margaret Harrais married a "Martin." Margaret's Martin also spoke with a thick accent, and like Martin Radovan was considered a "new immigrant." He had arrived from Riga, Latvia, at age twenty-three, attended college in Seattle, and headed to the Dawson goldfields after 1897. Margaret, who married him in 1920,

Martin and Augusta at Dan Creek

Mrs. Radovan, ca. 1929. Augusta (right) and perhaps Mrs. Price (left) out for a social snowshoe at Dan Creek. Courtesy of Jim Edwards.

commented to a friend before the ceremony that if she did decide to marry Martin, she would have to decide "to marry Alaska, too."[156] This was a sentiment undoubtedly shared by Augusta—and arguably any miner's wife at the time. During her eight years in McCarthy, Margaret Harrais taught school and, to the chagrin of McCarthy's hard-drinking parents, she instilled in the local children the principles of temperance. Through her organizing efforts, Margaret proudly witnessed the first female jurors perform their public duty, and she continued her involvement with the WCTU, accepting the position of president of Alaska's chapter in the mid-1920s.[157]

As Augusta's relationships with the other miners' wives showed, these pioneer women did not spend all of their time isolated in a cabin. They had public and social lives in which they organized everything from entertainment to morality. Even in Dan Creek, rules dictated social behavior representative of the times. Augusta belonged to a local bookclub, which read titles such as *Thou Israel* and *The Diary of Jean Evarts: The Business Man of Syria*, both written

Martin and Augusta at Dan Creek

in the 1920s by Charles Francis Stocking, and *Tamerlane: The Earth Shaker* by Harold Lamb.[158] On one occasion in March 1931, Augusta called on Mrs. Davis, but "Mrs. Price said she thought that she might be asleep, and that I had better not go and disturb her so I didn't." Concerned that she had not shown proper etiquette, Augusta added, "I hope she does not think that I passed her up on purpose, for I did not."[159] Likewise, on May 25, Augusta had expected friends to visit for a few days, but apparently they changed their minds. Noticeably upset by their display of bad manners, Augusta expressed a rare outburst of emotion in her journal that day:

> *At ten they all left for Price's camp. They were suppose to stay with me 3 or 4 days and imagine my surprise—they said they had to go back to town tomorrow after having dinner at Price's camp at one. I am suppose[d] to go down too but that is too much to ask of one who has been handed such a jolt. Rather a relief though, but I wouldn't let on...they will never be asked again. (Although they invited themselves this time).*[160]

Augusta often walked the road connecting McCarthy with Dan and May Creeks. She occasionally accepted a ride from passing cars. Here, operator of the Nizina Roadhouse, Jim Murie, and fellow passenger stop to check out the sights near May Creek during a 1938 road trip. John Cone Collection, WRST.

Because of the difference in socialization and life experience, men and women did not see the world identically. When Martin recorded his daily activities, he documented information useful to him. For example, he recorded information such as the length of his tunnel and types of mineral he uncovered that day. His notebook (after 1935) contained information such as social security numbers and travel itineraries. Martin hardly mentions life beyond mining.[161] Augusta, on the other hand, wrote about topics significant to her. That often meant the coming and goings of Nizina society. On December 31, 1930, she wrote, "I went down town saw Mrs. Hellenrich and the boys—and Mrs. Hubrick and Harte and his wife. The asst[ant] district attor[ney] came up yesterday to see about Dan Pearson who killed himself."[162] Two days later she noted that Mrs. Harrais gave a birthday dinner for her husband. "District attor[ney] and Barretts were invited." Although some might call it gossip, Augusta's depictions of residents and their activities provide a clearer idea of community life, the community's rules, and the active role that women played in organizing that community.

Martin and Augusta at Dan Creek

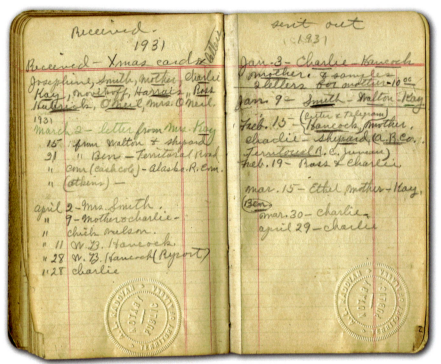

Another journal entry lists Christmas cards the Radovans received in 1931. Note the "A.L. Radovan public notary" imprint. Martin Radovan Private Collection.

Also present in Augusta's diary is a picture of how the communities were linked. On the way to town from Dan Creek, for example, Martin and Augusta stayed in roadhouses, which, among other uses, served as hubs of the community's social network. Many of Augusta's journal entries underscore the socialization conducted at these places, particularly the Nizina Roadhouse run by Jim and Tess Murie. On December 29, 1930, she wrote, "Martin and I are going to town. We stayed at the R[oad] H[ouse] and had lunch. Dusty and his wife were there. We reached town at 6 o'clock. Murre [Murie] brought in Dusty and his wife [Tess] right after us. We got some food from the store and went to Blackburn."[163] Likewise, on May 19, 1931 she wrote, "Got up early straightened things up, left at 11 for town. No mail train came in. I walked to Mile 3 saw Martin gave him note to sign for bill. Murri [Murie] caught up with me—I rode to R[oad] H[ouse] had lunch then to Dan Creek on Murie's truck—then home."[164]

Martin and Augusta often stopped at the Nizina Roadhouse while on their way to or from "town." This photo shows Jim Murie, his wife Tess, and an unidentified man posing in front of the Nizina Roadhouse, ca. 1938. Ethel Lecount Collection, WRST.

Martin and Augusta at Dan Creek

Always in the backdrop of Augusta and Martin's day-to-day life was their reliance upon the outside world. Beside trucks and trains, she described airplanes as necessary modes of modern transportation, noting that "First and second class mail came to McCarthy by airplane,"[165] and hinted at the work of the Alaska Road Commission expanding roads and bridges into the district.[166] Through those various modes of transportation, town stores were stocked with processed canned foods prepared by an industrial network of farmers, meat packers, canners, label makers, advertisers, and retail sales people that connected the Nizina Mining District to workers and environments across the United States. Martin and Augusta consumed local foods on occasion, but not enough natural resources were available to sustain the Nizina's growing population. On April 17, 1931, Augusta wrote, "Martin went to Kennecott…Got our groceries there." In the bitter cold month of February, Augusta mentioned that she received "six lemons," a citrus fruit grown in places like California and Florida.[167] And when bad weather prevented the train's arrival, thus breaking the link to the industrial market, it sparked "a food shortage in town."[168] As Martin and Augusta purchased and prepared their canned bacon and beans, they helped to create linkages that connected Dan Creek to the larger national economy.

Reliable mail service was vital to the inhabitants of mining communities like Dan Creek. Photograph by Daniel Trepal, National Park Service, Radovan camp site, 2010.

Underscoring the couple's connection to the outside world was Augusta's constant writing about the mail service. The entire Nizina community seemed to circulate around the postal service. On February 16, 1931, she wrote, "Stopped at R[oad] H[ouse] with mail also Price's camp where we had tea. Mrs. Price gave us some doughnuts to take home. They were nice. Had mail for them. Also had mail for Lou." On March 7, Augusta wrote, "I dreamed of El[ves] last night. It means news of some kind of letters." Indeed, it was not elves providing the mail service to Dan Creek, but rather a massive government-run network that depended upon steamships, railroads, trucks, airplanes, even dog teams to deliver the mail.

Martin and Augusta's well-being seemed almost contingent upon the mail service—Martin because it allowed him to communicate with the mining industry and Bureau of Mines, which represented the corporate and government institutions that ultimately dictated his mining future, and Augusta because it not only provided her employment

The town of McCarthy in the 1930s represented the social, economic, and cultural norms of any small town in rural America. Russ Dow papers, Archives and Special Collections, Consortium Library, University of Alaska Anchorage, uaa-hmc-0396-14a-231.

Martin and Augusta at Dan Creek

Remains of Martin's Dan Creek cabin, date unknown. Martin Radovan Private Collection.

at one time or another, but allowed her to receive word from family living in Seattle and other places far from Alaska. On March 22 she noted deep concern about a registered letter to Mr. Hancock regarding mineral samples that had not yet been delivered: "Martin worked in Tun[nel] this morning....A letter from Ben telling us that our letter is still in Chitina and has been since Feb. 25 or 26. Chitina P[ost] M[aster] would not send registered letter by plane unless authorized by postal inspector. Don't know what effect it will have on [mining] deal."[169]

Instead of waiting weeks, even months, for a response, Augusta, in the age of electrification and instant communication, had access to a telephone, even at Dan Creek. "March 30. I went down to Price's and phoned Ben about our registered letter. It left Chitina the 17th. So it must have got the boat leaving 22nd of Mar."[170] As a one-time employee of the postal service, Augusta nevertheless grumbled, "Five weeks is a long time to hold back a registered letter." On a separate occasion the mail brought better news: "April 9. Martin went down Lou hollered for him. There was mail—letter from mamma and Charlie which were very cheerful and one from Chic Nelson—saying that Presley wanted to See Martin."[171]

Augusta and Martin were always seeking ways to stay financially afloat, for looming in the background of daily life in the Nizina district was the ominous presence of the Great Depression. On December 31, 1930, Martin went to Kennecott and "saw Engineer who complained of hard times." He was there to ask James McGavock, Kennecott's master mechanic, for a loan. Augusta's mother, Thora, was also experiencing hard times and needed money for her house payment. "Martin asked McGavock for $75.00," explained Augusta. "He insisted on a note signed by us both and no time limit—a call note. We won't take it. Martin got $50.00 from Al Grate without anything to be signed for which we bless him and will remember him."[172]

While hard times fell upon the entire Nizina district, Martin was able to acquire what others could not—a job that paid wages. In spite of Kennecott's gradual decline, it was still the region's chief employer, and it provided Martin with needed work. On April 17, 1931, Martin agreed to do the company's assessment work for a new road. Accordingly, he earned $200 from the company and another $400 from the Alaska Road Commission.[173] Likewise, a month after the Stock Market crashed in October 1929, the U.S. Census reported Augusta employed as a typist at an office, undoubtedly at Kennecott.[174] Both were doing what they could to keep their dreams alive.

Although Martin continued to work at Dan Creek until the 1970s, he totaled only somewhere between $5,000 and $6,000 from the "benches."[175] He told Gary Green that his only real pay dirt at Dan Creek was "two halves of the same gold nugget."[176] Perhaps it was not the typical prospector fairytale life, but Martin and Augusta's experience at Dan Creek was, nevertheless, typical. Together, their "ordinary mining life" helps us to better understand mining societies. Martin and Augusta did not live a solitary life, suspended from other people, modern goods, and services. On the contrary, Augusta paints for us a picture of two people fully engaged in early twentieth century American society and culture. They participated in a community that replicated most rural American towns. It was a place where both men and women played major roles. And their livelihood was dependent on an industrialized economy that, through various modes of transportation, communication, and distant markets, linked their life at Dan Creek to people and places throughout the world.

The Prospector and the Impossible Prospect at Glacier Creek
1929–1944

I started back, to the camp, got there tired, opened up a can of beans, cooked some coffee, spread my blankets under a big spruce tree so tired.... As I slept, a vision came to me clear as a blue print...I saw a great bed of ore in that mountain, a thousand feet in, true solid rock, on both sides of the canyon....The vision of my dream.

~Martin Radovan
Martin's Dream

MARTIN LAUNCHED HIS SEARCH FOR COPPER IN THE MID-1920S in a mountainous and rugged region, where Pleistocene ice left behind flat-bottomed, steep-sided valleys with intimidating walls and jagged peaks reaching 6,000 to 8,000 feet high.[177] As a prospector, Martin forded swift, treacherous glacial streams, and while exploring elevations at easily 3,000 feet and above, he avoided a litany of dangers, primarily threats due to snowslides, rockslides, and mudslides. Martin's explorations eventually brought him to the west side of Glacier Creek, where he started prospecting in a glaciated cirque surrounded by steep cliffs that towered to 9,000 feet. "I set out to stake my own claim up there," recalled Martin, "and it took all summer to make the trip."[178]

The Radovans established a camp at Glacier Creek, a tributary of the Chitistone, which in 1913 and 1914 was used as a corridor for stampeders heading to the Chisana gold fields and quite likely how Martin originally came to the gulch in the first place.[179] About four miles separate the Radovans' Glacier Creek camp from their cabin on upper Dan Creek.[180] In between, however, lay some of the most rugged terrain in the Nizina district. One USGS geologist sent to the Chitistone-Glacier Creek area commented that "The highest peaks, more than 8,000 feet, are between Dan Creek and Glacier Creek. All of the area except the highest peaks and ridges had been glaciated, and glaciers still exist in several valleys and on the ridge between Dan and Glacier Creeks."[181]

ABOVE: The south upper section of the Binocular prospect. Note part of Radovan's trail along the contact shelf. Geneva-Pacific Collection, National Park Service.

View south: Radovan Gulch, circa 1970s.
Geneva-Pacific Collection, National Park Service.

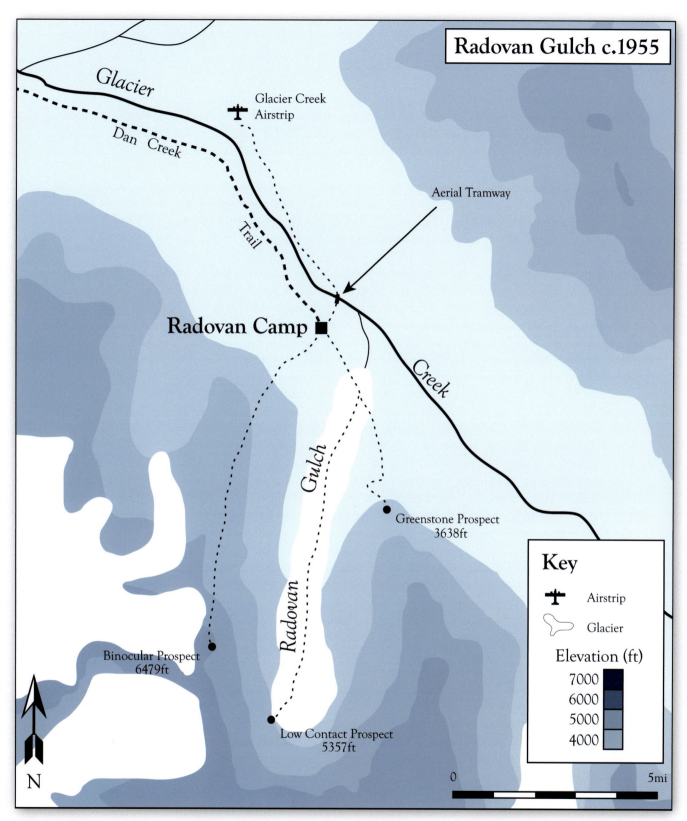

Radovan Gulch c.1955. Map by Daniel Trepal, National Park Service.

The Prospector and the Impossible Prospect at Glacier Creek

Forced to circumnavigate the mountains, Martin and Augusta followed about thirteen miles of foot and horse trails along the waterways. A well-traveled route took them to the mouth of Dan Creek; northward on a traversing trail on the flat along the east side of the Nizina River, eastward up the Chitistone River, and then back southward, up Glacier Creek drainage.[182] Spruce Point on the Nizina River and Peavine Bar on the Chitistone supported roadhouses, which served as temporary staging areas for portaging supplies. When the trail was in good shape, the distance between the two camps could be traveled in under a day, and if horses were used, it took only several hours.[183] Jim Edwards remembers that Martin "worked both properties, traveling back and forth on foot over river bars and through the brush several times each year."[184] The only other prospector in the area was Charles Nelson, who had discovered a promising copper deposit not far from Martin's camp in 1928.

Inspired by the success of the Kennecott Copper Corporation, Martin believed that he would find "the greatest bonanza of all times on Glacier Creek."[185] Underscoring his optimism was the presence of a large copper stain high on the face of a steep-walled recess in the same geologic formation—the Chitistone limestone—that held the Bonanza deposit. Martin's interest was shared by others, for the outcrop had intrigued prospectors for years. None had ever reached the stain, however, for its location on the cliff face made the prospect unreachable. The outcrops, therefore, had only been scanned with binoculars.[186] Territorial Mining inspector Earl Pilgrim explained in his *Report on Cooperative Mining Investigations* in 1931 that, because the surface ore exposures were "visible from a distance with the aid of binoculars, the outcrops were referred to as the "binocular prospect.""[187]

In 1929, the combination of Depression-era market stagnation and dwindling production due to the depletion of high-grade ore sources caused Kennecott, one of the richest copper mines in the world, to commence its decadal decline. At the time, however, Kennecott had made formidable efforts to revitalize operations and continued to seek new profitable discoveries in the Nizina district. That summer, Kennecott optioned Charles Nelson's claim on lower Glacier Creek. Interested in the Binocular Prospect as well, the company hired several expert European mountain climbers to reach the outcrop, but the cliff was too steep and the weather too volatile in 1929. As a result, the climbers left unsuccessful, and the prospect was deemed by all simply impossible.[188]

Meanwhile, a forty-seven-year-old man with absolutely no mountain climbing experience was also trying to figure out how to reach Binocular. Each day Martin studied the impossibly steep cliff-face. "I sat down on the small rock," recalled Martin, "and looking up, almost three thousand feet, underneath [the] over-hanging mountain." Feeling defeated by Binocular, Martin left the gulch for the day. Then he remembered the advice from his mother—*to use his head and save himself a lot of walking*. That night he dreamed about Binocular, and figured out a way to reach it.

The dream inspired Martin to ascend the mountain from the northeastern side of the gulch. The next day, he started by climbing a steep switchback trail from behind his cabin until he reached a hanging valley with the remnant of a small glacier. Passing just to the south of the glacier, at an elevation of 6,480 feet, Martin crossed over the ridge into the gulch at the point where the Nikolai Greenstone makes contact with the Chitistone Limestone. With a 2,000 foot drop descending to the unnamed glacier below, and 1,000 feet of rock and ice hanging precariously above, Martin followed the narrow shelf atop the greenstone for over a mile. Describing his ascent to Binocular years later, Martin confided, "I felt guilty, to sneak in from behind."[189] In doing so, Martin became the first person to reach the Binocular Prospect.

Jim Edwards, one of the few people who ascended Binocular besides Martin, recalls that "In some places it [the path] is only a foot wide. At one point it passes under an overhanging glacier (which Martin called "the ice cream cone") and often large chunks of ice fall onto the trail."[190] Local Resident Loy Green was similarly amazed by Martin's feat: "Binocular's cliffs are almost vertical, and from base to top over 3000 feet."[191] Martin, however, appeared unfazed by the hazards the mountain presented: "A few bad places but not too bad," he recalled. "I came to a narrow point, face to face, with binocular prospect."[192]

The Prospector and the Impossible Prospect at Glacier Creek

Kennecott postcard, undated. Like the many prospectors who sought copper in the Wrangell Mountains, Martin was inspired by Kennecott's famed copper deposits. Martin Radovan Private Collection.

Martin's exploitation of the Binocular Prospect was so remarkable that those familiar with the vertical environment questioned his achievement. "As Martin was alone with no one to witness his activities," wrote Green, "no one knows how he did the seemingly impossible feat."[193] But Martin was not alone. He had Augusta with him. With her help, he cut steps hundreds of feet along the face of the cliff. "For twenty-six days, I worked hard, from twelve to sixteen hours a day," recalled Martin. They worked until the trail reached a point two hundred feet below the copper outcrops. From there, Martin scaled the wall, using ropes and steel spikes driven into rock crevices.[194] The accomplishment instantly made Martin a local hero among regional miners.

By 1930, word of Martin's Binocular conquest had circulated throughout Alaska's mining districts. Investigator Earl Pilgrim was one of the first to recognize the prospect's precipitous location, noting that "The surface outcrops were considered inaccessible...until Mr. Radovan's resourcefulness solved the problem of constructing a trail to the locality."[195] Newspaper reports described an "eleven foot wide, solid vein of high grade copper," uncovered by Martin Radovan.[196] The *Alaska Weekly* declared, "New Glacier Creek Strike is Important," noting that Asa

Martin ascended Binocular from the northeastern side of the gulch, following a steep switchback trail from behind his Glacier Creek cabin. Photograph by Samson Ferreira, National Park Service, 2007.

The Prospector and the Impossible Prospect at Glacier Creek

Baldwin, a Seattle mining engineer, had "no doubt that the Glacier Creek lime formation will show another big copper producer."[197] "Radovan unaided...," boasted the paper, "...has built trails and done development work on one of the most rugged pieces Mother Nature has ever tossed up. A precipice thousands of feet high with overhanging glacier, paths like mountain goat trails, upon which in many places, one has to crawl on hands and knees, is the game that Radovan played to prove the riches hidden away in the most inaccessible of places ever built on this universe."[198]

That same summer, the *Fairbanks Daily News-Miner* reported: "Solid mountain of copper believed have been found." As with the *Alaska Weekly*, the *News-Miner* also pointed out that Radovan's prospect was located "in the same geological formation as the Kennecott mine," and justified the construction of a short spur that could be "made accessible to the present Copper River railroad."[199]

After the Binocular feat, Martin and Augusta focused on establishing their summer camp on the narrow floodplain, tucked between the south bank of Glacier Creek and a steep mountain, covered by a sentinel of alders, birches, and spruce. By 1930, they had built a small cabin measuring 13 feet by 8 feet, constructed with milled planks and set on a foundation of cobblestone from the nearby creek.[200] Their door included a manufactured key latch and enameled knob reminiscent of those used in homes in the pre-1920s.[201] At one point they built an addition to the cabin, which probably served as a kitchen and storage for sundry items.[202]

Martin's trail crossed over the ridge into the gulch at the point where the Nikolai Greenstone makes contact with the Chitistone Limestone. Geneva-Pacific Collection, National Park Service.

"Finds Solid Vein High Grade Copper: Solid Mountain Copper Believed Have Been Found—Is Accessible to Copper River Road." *Fairbanks Daily News-Miner*, August 28, 1931.

Map of Martin Radovan's claims. Martin Radovan Private Collection.

The Radovans began to live at their small cabin at Glacier Creek for longer periods of time, and Martin, who had been employed to do assessment work for Kennecott that spring, quit his job so that he could spend even more time in the gulch.[203] The couple moved their belongings from their cabin on Dan Creek to Glacier Creek for the season, using horses to haul their provisions. In spring 1930, Augusta wrote in her journal that "Late afternoon Martin went down and saw [J.J.] Price about paying for horses and taking mail into town." On May 12, Martin constructed a distinctive cache. It was an A-framed structure, elevated on four 6- to 8-inch diameter spruce log posts, about twelve feet tall. He situated the cache in the trees behind the cabin, near the base of the mountain. The following day, Augusta and Martin "stored everything in the cache," and then returned to Dan Creek for another load.[204] Besides the cabin and cache, they also constructed an outhouse, a gabled-roof structure for storage, and a water system for collecting drinking water from a small stream behind the cabin.[205]

The Prospector and the Impossible Prospect at Glacier Creek

Martin and Augusta Radovan's Glacier Creek Cabin built ca. 1929. Photographed during an NPS site survey by the National Park Service, 1994.

By 1931, Martin and Augusta had staked thirty claims around the Binocular Prospect, known as the Triassic claims, 1-30. As regional and territorial papers waxed enthusiastically about the Binocular Prospect's discovery, Martin turned his full attention to its development. Each morning, Martin rose, made coffee and pancakes, and headed into the gulch to work on the Binocular Prospect. He loaded his pack with the necessary gear for a day of prospecting. The intimidating nature of the terrain he had to cross dictated that he travel lightly. His mining equipment consisted of the most basic hand tools in use: a small sledge (hammer), a pair of two-foot starter (drill) steels, several sticks of explosive, blasting caps, and a length of fuse. He may have made a long, slender spoon out of whatever materials he had available in camp (tin cans, wire, and so forth) to use in cleaning out the drill holes in the rock. He may also have brought a light source, or (due to the shallowness of the prospect) relied on natural light to illuminate his work. Apart from these tools, only the most basic items of gear—a handkerchief, pocketknife, matches, water, some canned food, and of course his pancakes wrapped in paper, rounded out Martin's mining equipment.

Once packed, Martin began to climb the slope immediately south of his camp, up the western shoulder of Radovan Gulch. The terrain was at first wooded, eventually yielding to shorter shrubs, grasses, and moss as the elevation increased. After a few switchbacks, Martin reached the bare greenstone bedrock. Working his way to near the top of the ridge, he picked his way through this jagged volcanic rock. In some places he probably made a few minor improvements to make his way easier: crude steps blasted with dynamite on a steep section, perhaps with a rope as a handhold.

After a mile or so working his way through the greenstone, Martin reached the contact – the point at which the deposit of lighter-colored limestone lying over the greenstone created a visible line where the two came into contact. The terrain at the contact was eroded so that, along the sheer cliff that formed the sides of the gulch, a small ledge of greenstone projected out from below the limestone. It was just wide enough for a person to tentatively scramble

The Prospector and the Impossible Prospect at Glacier Creek

along the treacherous, loose scree. Martin had improved this ledge with a few handholds and ropes. The last 150 feet of the journey consisted of a vertical climb on a rope ladder from the contact ledge to the stain in the rock.

Once at the stain, Martin used his steel and sledge to drill holes in the rock. Turning the steel after each strike created a fairly round hole. Once they were deep enough to hold a charge, Martin cleaned the holes of loose rock using his spoon and primed his explosives. He stuck a blasting cap on the end of a section of fuse and inserted this into the stick of explosive. The primed charge was then placed in the drilled hole (he might "shoot" several holes at a time), the fuse lit with a match, and as it burned, Martin gingerly climbed out of the way as quickly as possible. After working in this manner for some time, he had a small tunnel with a ledge on which he continued to work. His goal was not necessarily to find the ore body itself, but to extract samples from the rock showing promising enough geology to attract the interest of large, well-capitalized mining companies, such as Kennecott.

After a day's worth of work, Martin climbed back down to the contact and made his way back towards camp, perhaps with a sample of ore if he found anything that looked promising. His drill steels would be dull and in need of sharpening. After having worked this prospect for a few years, Martin hauled a mattress and perhaps a few other small bits of gear to the ledge of the prospect, allowing him to work on the tunnel for several days at a time. Over the next ten years, Martin devoted nearly all his time and energy to tunneling towards his mountain of copper, attempting to realize his dream.

By 1933, however, USGS geologists were unconvinced that Martin had indeed discovered the next Kennecott-style "Bonanza." The Alaska Director at USGS, Philip Smith, cautioned prospectors and investors alike: "It must be remembered that the mines near Kennecott, which have contributed perhaps 90 percent of the Alaska copper, have been mining a unique deposit, not comparable with any other known deposit in the world, so that inevitably their mineral wealth is being depleted and there is no justification for expecting that their loss will be offset by new discoveries of equally marvelous lodes."[206]

Still, Martin remained hopeful. In 1935 he sent a letter to the U.S. Geological Survey in Fairbanks. "Gentlemen," he wrote, "I am sending three samples to be assayed. They are from the Triassic group of Claims on Glacier Creek." In the letter, he also noted that the "Augusta Radovan dike" was discovered that summer. It was covered with so much ice and snow that Martin had to pick about 30 feet of ice to get to it. The location of the dike was at the base of what he named Louise Mountain, to the left limit of Glacier Creek, about 125 feet above the greenstone/limestone contact. "Would like to know," inquired Martin, "if dike is Porphyry or not."[207]

Meanwhile, as Martin's mining fate appeared to be in the hands of an absentee agency, the Nizina Mining District's economic producer, the Kennecott Copper Corporation, began, as the USGS warned, to show signs of decline as the Great Depression continued to stall the world's economy. The mine, railroad, and exploration work kept a majority of the area's population employed, but according to the corporation's annual report forecast, the mill would eventually be closed if no new ore bodies could be found.[208] In 1931, copper prices fell to 5 cents a pound, and Kennecott Copper Corporation reported a loss of $2 million that year.[209] A reprise appeared possible in 1935 with the establishment of the National Recovery Administration that increased the price of copper from 4.5 cents to 9 cents a pound, but later that year, the Supreme Court declared the Act unconstitutional, and the price of copper declined by 1 cent per pound.[210]

Besides plummeting prices, other factors contributed to the decline. By the mid-1930s, Kennecott's ore was nearly mined out. But the Kennecott Copper Corporation owned a huge mine in Chile and had acquired the Utah Copper Company in 1935, which reduced exponentially its dependency on its Alaskan mines. In addition, a shipping strike, which started in November and December on the Pacific Coast and lasted until 1937, disrupted

The Prospector and the Impossible Prospect at Glacier Creek

transportation of Kennecott's ore. The final straw came when the territorial legislature voted to tax all mining enterprises in Alaska.[211] Even though Kennecott produced more copper in 1937 than in the previous eight years, no new ore bodies had been discovered, so the corporation decided "to discontinue all operation at Kennecott in that later part of 1938 upon completion of the mining of the remaining tonnage of ore."[212]

Following the closure of the mines, Kennecott abandoned the Copper River & Northwestern Railway. Then, the annual washout of the Copper River Bridge at Chitina cut off the Nizina district. USGS's Philip Smith recognized the closure as a deathblow to Alaska mining. "The record of these great mines marks a series of brilliant achievements in the history of Alaska mining, and their closing forms a distinct loss not only to the mining industry but also to the development of the whole territory."[213] As the town of McCarthy folded soon thereafter, "for Martin and Augusta," notes Edwards, "the isolation was almost complete."[214]

During those years, two family deaths drew the Radovans from their seclusion. Augusta had traveled stateside before, presumably to visit her family in the Pacific Northwest. In 1925, for example, the *McCarthy Weekly News* reported that, "Mrs. Radovan leaves on the morning train for a trip Outside on November 28. The trip is expected to last for a couple of months."[215] Augusta left Alaska for a second time when her brother Charlie, at age fifty-two, died of a cerebral hemorrhage on April 22, 1934.[216] At the time, Charlie was working as a tile setter and living with their mother at the same address in southwest Seattle.[217] Then, in 1940, the *Daily News-Miner* listed Mrs. Martin Radovan as a "Valdez passenger," sailing on the Alaska Steamship Company vessel the S.S. *Baranof*, en route to Alaska from Seattle.[218] Augusta had gone to Seattle because on August 2, 1939, her eighty-year-old mother, Thora, had died.[219]

Four years later, Augusta was in Valdez where she too succumbed to a cerebral hemorrhage. Augusta, a type II diabetic, was admitted into the Valdez Community Hospital on July 26, and died three days later. Although official records state that she was sixty, Augusta was actually sixty-four when she died. Martin, who apparently was not with Augusta when she passed, signed her death certificate on August 14, 1944. Where she was buried, however, remains a mystery. No record of her being buried at Valdez exists—neither a headstone nor any written records.[220] Given his Catholic background and devotion to his wife, Martin surely would have provided Augusta a proper place to rest. Those who knew Martin claim that he charted a plane, likely from Merle "Mudhole" Smith whose Cordova Air Service served the mining districts in Wrangell Mountain region, and had Augusta flown back to Glacier Creek, where he buried her somewhere near their cabin.[221] Years later Theodore Van Zelst of the Van Zelst Group, a prospecting company that held the Glacier Creek claims after Martin died, wrote a letter to Martin's niece, Katherine Cesare, in 1985, in which he confirmed antidotal speculation:

> *Those who worked in the area after Martin Radovan passed away and who had a chance to inspect the area around his cabins, believed that she may be buried in the woods behind the cabin, along Glacier Creek. For some years there was evidence of a pathway leading out to the back of the cabin that led to "nowhere." Those who knew Martin believe that this may have been the location of his wife's grave.*[222]

Augusta Radovan death certificate, July 29, 1944. Office of Vital Statistics, State of Alaska.

The Prospector and the Impossible Prospect at Glacier Creek

Some believe that Martin buried Augusta at an unmarked site near the cache behind their Glacier Creek cabin. A letter to Radovan's family from Theodore Van Zelst, a Geneva Pacific geologist, revealed that his team had discovered a possible grave site, indicating truth to the rumors. The grave, however, has yet to be found in the overgrowth surrounding the cabin. Augusta's final resting place, therefore, continues to be a mystery. Photograph by Samson Ferreria, National Park Service, 2007.

Martin and Augusta spent thirty years together in the Nizina district, and according to Jim Edwards, "found much happiness in the freedom of their great mountain country."[223] Throughout the decades, the couple's relationship was tied to their seasonal movement between two camps and the cherished partnership that grew strong over many years. The Radovans' marriage remained a solid and steady reality for Martin, but with the loss of Augusta in 1944—the person who supported and shared his vision and his dreams—Martin's story took a drastic turn.

By the end of World War II, Alaska's mining industry, like Martin's marriage, had changed significantly. Besides the fact that the driving force of copper mining in the Nizina district had closed its mines in 1938, most geologists agreed that the Kennecott-type ore that supplied the mill town was unique and no more significant copper lodes existed beyond the Bonanza Ridge. In 1943, USGS investigator Don Miller visited the Nizina district and reported that "None of the known deposits (including those at Radovan Gulch) is believed to offer sufficient promise of significant production or profit to warrant the cost of reestablishing a practicable means of transportation to the district solely for the copper."[224] As mining technology and methodology became more professionalized and expensive, the industry and government alike saw little use for the intimate knowledge acquired through years of prospecting by men like Martin Radovan.

The Lone Prospector: Life after Gussie
1944–1951

For all his strength of character and physical endurance, he is, with animals, one of the kindest and gentlest of men.

~James "Jim" Edwards on Martin Radovan
Alaska Sportsman, 1965

"Whenever anything moved there in my valley, whether it be man or animal, Bootsie would scratch some bare boards next to my stove pipe until I came out to see what it was," said Radovan. "He was better than the best watchdog." "Animals know when you like them, they sense it," he said. "I think more of them than I do of myself."

~Martin Radovan,
Quoted in "Venerable Sourdough," *Anchorage Daily Time*, 1972

IN THE YEARS AFTER AUGUSTA'S DEATH, Martin made a lasting mark on the Nizina's copper landscape, primarily with his name. By 1943, locals began calling the glacier-filled cirque valley on Glacier Creek "Radovan Gulch" and named the glacier that filled its floor "Radovan Glacier."[225] Although he still maintained his Dan Creek residence, Martin started staying at the Glacier Creek camp for longer periods of time, sometimes even remaining the winter. Season after season, Martin carried on with his prospecting work at Binocular, but even though his faith in the prospect remained strong, his patience had waned. When no ore body materialized, he began to redirect his exploratory activities. Between 1945 and 1951, Martin spent a majority of his time developing new prospects. He made a second foot-trail that paralleled the glacier's lateral moraine to its steep terminus, and he started working at a site about 150 feet above the contact zone in the northwest corner of the gulch. Whereas Binocular was considered a "high-contact deposit," because this new prospect was located where a prominent fault had dropped the limestone-greenstone contact 1,000 feet vertically, it was fittingly called "Low-Contact."[226]

ABOVE: The ladder to the Low-Contact prospect, circa 1955. Courtesy of Jim Edwards.

Martin climbing a ladder near Low-Contact, date unknown. The sheer rock face is comprised of Nikolai Greenstone below and Chitistone Limestone high overhead. Geneva-Pacific Collection, National Park Service.

The Lone Prospector: Life after Gussie

Martin had discovered the Low-Contact deposit back in the mid-1930s while prospecting near the lower part of the fault. In 1940, the Bureau of Mines established a program designed to aid exploratory development leading to the expansion of domestic copper output. The start of World War II ignited an unprecedented consumption of the ore for the manufacturing of airplanes, tanks, and munitions, which caused a major copper shortage in the United States. Virtually all civilian needs for copper were cut off by 1945.[227]

Meanwhile, word of Martin's Binocular discovery had made its way to the Bureau, and by the mid-1940s, concerns representing the federal government started visiting Radovan Gulch to investigate Martin's claims. Besides Binocular, Martin also told a mine inspector about a four-foot vein of "dense, hard, metallic sulfides" exposed in the bottom of the narrow, steep ravine at the head of the gulch.[228] Martin's description of the Low-Contact prospect interested the Bureau's man, but not long after Martin had made the discovery, a snowslide covered the vein in ice and rock and prevented the inspector from validating Martin's assertions regarding the claim.

Part of the problem was that the location of the Low-Contact prospect, although it was lower in altitude, was no less treacherous than the Binocular, which sat looming high above on the north cliff-face. A major obstacle was that Martin could only access the Low-Contact prospect in July and August. During the warm months, melting ice and rock avalanches broke from the perpetual ice cap, crashing down upon the narrow ravine almost every hour of the day, making tunneling work extremely dangerous.[229] On a separate inspection, a USGS geologist described the perilous nature of the work environment at Martin's Low-Contact tunnels: "Frequent rock showers down the fault zone make it hazardous to venture to this prospect and force one to take refuge in the tunnels in the ice filling the lower part of the cut." He added that "it is unlikely that a lone prospector will ever be able to examine safely the outcrops in the zone above."[230]

The geological conclusions at the time were not promising. In 1943 a USGS geologist visited Radovan Gulch and pointed out that all of the ore bodies supplying Kennecott were located in Chitistone Limestone and the principal sulfide mineral was chalcocite. The Radovan deposits, though also in the limestone, differed in that bornite and pyrite were more abundant than chalcocite.[231] The geologist concluded that "no significant quantity of copper minerals was found" at the two exploratory tunnels at Low-Contact and that the outcrops at Binocular "apparently do not contain a significant quantity of copper." The agency did not dismiss the prospect entirely, however, postulating that "they may indicate the presence of copper-bearing material of higher grade at depth."[232]

Blasting caps. Martin Radovan Private Collection.

Undeterred, Martin, now well into his sixties, continued the search for the vein he had discovered years before at the head of the gulch. He first chipped steps in the ice out to the site where he believed the ore was located. Then, in the middle of the slide area, he drove a tunnel into the snow and frozen muck. He removed all the rock by hand and drilled his blast holes with a hand steel and single-jack hammer.[233] Every few days he had to remove loose rock from the hole. Since everything was done by hand, Martin could only enter the tunnel on hands and knees. Jim Edwards later explained that the gulch's rugged environment was nearly impossible to overcome: "Because of the time it took to tramp four miles on snowshoes to the site, climb 40 feet up the loose snow slide, do the drilling and blasting, and return home, progress was slow. He could advance his tunnel only about six inches a day." Adding to the slow pace of work was the extreme weather. Each summer, melting ice, rocks, and mud filled the tunnel, then winter froze it solid. The cycle of freeze and thaw rendered most forward progress moot. Still, Martin, who was never daunted by the task at hand, simply started a new tunnel the following spring and continued to dig, weather permitting, until the deep snow of autumn fell. Over the years, Martin dug a total of sixteen tunnels at

The Lone Prospector: Life after Gussie

Low-Contact, with one measuring more than 125 feet.[234]

Besides the Binocular and Low-Contact prospects, Martin had also discovered the Greenstone prospect. By 1943, he held twelve of the thirty claims he had staked on the north side of Radovan Gulch between 1929 and 1931. On July 30, 1948, Martin staked a lode claim of 1,500 feet long by 600 feet wide along the Augusta Radovan vein, which he had named for his wife back in 1935.[235] The deposit was located on the gulch's southwest slope, 4,000 feet up in the Nikolai Greenstone, approximately 3,000 feet below the contact. Martin aptly named it the "Greenstone Prospect." To get to Greenstone, Martin crossed the gulch's active glacier and then followed a switchback trail up the slope of the mountain. Over time, he staked other claims on the vein. In 1948, he added the "Agusta" [sic] claim, the "Boots" claim, the "Ki-Ki" claim, the "Pongo Boy" claim, and the "Triassic No. 31" and "Triassic No. 32" claims to his holdings.[236]

Martin marked the location of his three prospects—Binocular, Low-Contact, and Greenstone (just off the photograph). He used the photograph to possibly interest potential investors. Martin Radovan Private Collection.

When he successfully avoided the risks of his prospecting, Martin sent geologists samples from his work. One of his samples from the Augusta vein was assayed at 78 percent copper.[237] After investigation of the mine in 1951, geologists conceded that the Greenstone produced some native copper, but determined that the ore deposit was essentially chalcocite. Moreover, contrary to Martin's beliefs, they concluded that little similarity existed between the mineralization at Radovan's Greenstone and Low-Contact prospects and the Kennecott ore bodies, postulating that the minerals were deposited at different periods in geological time.[238] Still, evidence of copper minerals existed at Radovan Gulch. As a result, investigators recommended that the fault between Greenstone and Low-Contact "should be prospected in detail, and those sulphide occurrences near the zone warrant exploratory work."[239] Martin was more than happy to accommodate them.

The 1950s was an extraordinary time of national growth, but in many ways, Martin maintained a nineteenth-century preindustrial intimacy with the ecosystem that surrounded him. He employed simple, non-mechanical tools, had a "practical knowledge" of the gulch's geology (in other words, he knew what minerals to look for), and through hard and dangerous work Martin not only engaged but overcame the barriers presented by the gulch's hazardous natural landscape. Unfortunately for Martin, the mining industry by World War II had placed a new emphasis on modern technology and expertise, supplied by academically trained, degree-holding engineers.[240] The copper industry, in particular, faced a reality that no other massive Kennecott-type lodes were going to be found in the Wrangell Mountains. If copper was to be discovered, it would surely be much lower-grade mineral deposits. To reap profits then, far more complex—and expensive—exploratory mining techniques needed to be implemented. Though more efficient, this rational approach to mining valued guidance from engineers and other scientists, and consequently, the industry began to marginalize practical knowledge and day-to-day experience of prospectors like Martin Radovan.[241]

Still, season after season Martin scoured the steep slopes that surrounded the gulch for copper while the rest of the world seemed to pass him by. Americans across the nation were utilizing the commodities, conveniences, and opportunities brought by the postwar economy, yet in the Nizina district, the population had plummeted to numbers not seen in fifty years.[242] Kennecott was abandoned, Blackburn had long-since vanished, and McCarthy remained a shell of its former self with only a handful of residents remaining. Martin probably felt that he was entirely alone in his mountain wilderness.

Being alone presented Martin with many obstacles. One of the biggest hurdles Martin faced during his more solitary years was getting himself, as well as his supplies, across Glacier Creek in the summertime. On hot days, glacier melt causes the creek to flow swiftly at a depth of six to eight feet. Because the river changed its channel often, a bridge was no solution. Martin solved this problem by building a tram across the creek. According to his friend Jim Edwards, Martin obtained permission to use a spool of three-quarter-inch steel cable that had been left on a bar six miles from his camp. "Alone and unaided," explained Edwards, "he cut off about 400 feet of the cable, rolled it up, and hauled it the six miles upriver on a hand sled."[243] With only some rope and a single block, Martin stretched the cable a span of 325 feet across the creek.

The system Martin used to tighten the cable underscored the type of resourcefulness he employed while living by himself. In an *Alaska Sportsman* article entitled "Martin Radovan," Edwards described his friend's innovative system: "With one end of the cable fastened solidly in the ground, the other end was passed over a post and tied around a log. The log was free to move up and down in a pit, but was held away from the pull of the cable by spacers placed against

Martin crosses Glacier Creek on his handmade tram. Courtesy of Jim Edwards.

The Lone Prospector: Life after Gussie

"Martin's Tram," date unknown. Martin Radovan Private Collection.

another log solidly embedded in the side of the pit. When a deck was laid on the moveable log and piled with a ton or two of rocks, it would pull the cable a few inches over the post. The cable then was secured with a rope while the rocks could be removed, the log retied, and the operation repeated."[244] Accordingly, Martin's ingenuity became legendary throughout the Nizina district.

It was also about this time that Martin became known for his unusual companions. Indeed, Martin may have been alone at Radovan Gulch, but he was never lonely. Continuing a passion he shared with Augusta at Dan Creek, Martin fed the local wildlife, and the wildlife responded by providing Martin with constant companionship. He cooked rice and raisins for the local birds and fed them several times a day.[245] A flock of gray jays became so tame that they would land on his fingers and take food straight from his mouth. Besides the jays, Martin fed Canadian sparrows, squirrels, and bears. His most beloved companion was a fox named "Bootsie," who Martin apparently taught to pull a string connected to a camera, that took photographs of the lone prospector.[246] Martin's recollection of the story of Bootsie was retold in an *Anchorage Daily Times* article from 1972:

"I first saw him one morning when I went down to the river to knock a hole in the ice for water," said Radovan. "I looked up to see him standing 15 feet away. He ran in a big circle, about 200 feet, and returned to the spot where he started." I said to him, 'Are you hungry, boy? Come with me for something to eat.'" The fox followed Radovan into his cabin, where he immediately jumped up on Radovan's bed. Bootsie Boy became a member of the family, and would not go out of sight unless Radovan was with him. With the snow level up to the roof, it was easy for the fox to walk up there. He slept close to the stovepipe, where it was warm.[247]

Martin's memories of Bootsie suggest a relationship that was extremely meaningful. Underscoring the importance of the relationships he formed with the wildlife was the names he assigned his Greenstone claims: Second only to his wife, Augusta, was the "Boots" claim named for his pet fox, Bootsie; then he named the "Ki-Ki claim after the jays, and finally, "Pongo Boy," named for the bear he fed and befriended at his Glacier Creek camp.

James Edwards recalled that when Martin first met Bootsie, he had fed the fox "a can of clams," and the animal "moved right indoors to stay."[248] The fact that Martin lured Bootsie with canned food also suggests that, as isolated as Martin appeared at Radovan Gulch, he did not exist beyond the reach of American industrial life. Martin's independence, while resourceful, was not enough for him to survive completely on his own. In order to live at Glacier Creek, especially throughout the winter months, Martin remained linked to the outside world through a network of steamships, roads, and airplanes. Although he hauled his own supplies up the trail from Dan Creek and cut his own cordwood to heat his cabin, he still ate processed, mass-produced food canned by the razor clam and salmon canning industry in Cordova, or most likely, shipped north from farms and industrial cities located in the lower 48.

Counterclockwise: "Martin kissing his Ki-Ki birds." Martin took the photograph himself using a string tied to his camera. Martin Radovan Private Collection.

"Boots Boy," date unknown. Martin Radovan Private Collection.

"Martin with Boots Boy." Note the string that Martin tied to his camera in order to capture the shot. Martin Radovan Private Collection.

Martin's Camera. Courtesy of Emily Aiken Campbell. Photograph by the author, 2011.

The Lone Prospector: Life after Gussie

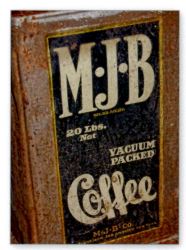

MJB Coffee. Photograph by Samson Ferreira, National Park Service, Radovan's Camp, 2007.

Martin consumed *Skippy* peanut butter, canned tomato sauce, and *Smucker's* blackberry jam. He drank *Nestlé's Quik* chocolate drink mix and *Hills Bros.* coffee. He prepared and seasoned his food with a variety of condiments, such as dried mustard, *French's* mustard, olive oil, savory salt, black pepper, soy sauce, and *Tiger Brand* curry powder. Meals were consumed on a complete stock of dishes, saucers, coffee cups, lunch pails, knives, forks, and spoons, and were cooked using pots, pans, cheese graters, muffin tins, and baking and roasting pans. His kitchen shelves were lined with wallpaper and contained sundry cooking utensils such as a wash pan and coffee pot. Keeping himself groomed was also important. He used *Aqua Velva* cologne, various lotions, and *Wildroot Cream Oil* hair tonic. He owned a .22 handgun and a 30-06 caliber rife, and maintained an ample supply of flashlight batteries.[249] Although Martin appeared to live a life of solitude at Glacier Creek, his clothes, supplies, and even the materials for his cabin connected Martin to distant people and places.

With the CR & NW Railway out of commission, Martin adjusted to new and far more complicated systems of transportation. In 1945, for fifteen dollars a ton, Martin could have his provisions hauled to Chitina, and then for another fifteen a ton, to McCarthy. Steamships brought supplies from the Outside to Valdez, where they were freighted 120 miles to Chitina by truck. There, small "gas speeders" hauled freight to McCarthy over the old railroad which, due to a lack of maintenance, was almost impassable. Complicating ground transportation were floods that destroyed the Copper River Bridge at Chitina and the Kennicott Bridge near McCarthy. A small boat or tram were at times the only available methods for crossing. Once across, a truck could still haul supplies to Dan Creek along the deteriorating old wagon road. Once goods finally arrived, Martin could then use a tractor or horses to carry supplies the remaining twenty miles up the Nizina and Chitistone valleys to Glacier Creek.[250]

Because ground transportation was so inefficient, a more popular mode of transportation was the airplane. Mail carriers had employed air transportation in the Nizina district by the end of the 1920s. The Alaska Road Commission constructed an airstrip near McCarthy Creek in 1927, making air transportation accessible to the area by the 1930s.[251] With the washout and lack of maintenance of both the Nizina River Bridge and the May Creek Road, those continuing to work in the Nizina Mining District were increasingly compelled to use airplanes to haul freight and transport ore across the rivers. In 1948, the Alaska Road Commission created a mile-long clearing near May Creek, used by Piper Cubs and C-47 cargo planes.[252] By 1951, a landing strip about 3,000 feet in length was constructed to facilitate cargo-carrying planes into the Glacier Creek area.

By the mid-1950s, Cordova Airlines included the Glacier Creek airstrip on its mail route. Martin could then have supplies flown out to him. Martin Radovan Private Collection.

The Lone Prospector: Life after Gussie

Local pilot Kenny Smith, Merle Smith's son and one of the few people who had contact with Martin during these years, remembers the prospector as "a tough old bird." According to Smith, Martin lived at Glacier Creek long enough that it became a certificated stop on the interior mail run, even though he was the only one there. The airstrip and little mail shack at Glacier Creek were on the east side of the creek, and Martin's camp and prospects were on the west side. Smith's memories of Martin indicate that, despite Martin's isolation, he held onto his connection with the outside world. Martin "couldn't meet the mail plane," recalled Smith, [so] "he left the outgoing mail in the cabin and we [Cordova Airlines bush pilots], in turn, left his mail and groceries there."[253] Smith remembered that Martin used to set his watch on the table with a note for the pilots to set the correct time when he would forget to wind it. Thus, instead of allowing the lightness and darkness of nature to govern his working hours, Martin conceded association with an industrial culture that viewed time as money.[254]

Martin would leave his watch at the mail shack at the Glacier Creek airstrip so that Cordova Airlines pilots could set the correct time. Martin Radovan Private Collection.

In spite of canned food and airstrips, Martin was still very much on his own. With only his pet Bootsie providing companionship, Martin remained the gulch's lone prospector and was as determined as ever to find his copper mountain. It was sometime in the early 1950s, in the latter part of fall, when Martin decided to hike to Low-Contact to look one last time for the copper vein. Feeling inspired, off he went, following the trail up the glacier, into the gulch's gut. On a final surveillance of the drift, he struck his pick into the cliff. As the arctic light slowly faded, Martin managed to pack out a few good samples. He placed them in his pocket and picked his way down the glacier. To quicken his pace home, Martin chose to slide down the ravine on his backside and, using his increasing momentum, jump a crevasse that had formed where the melting glacier had separated from the stagnant ice. After a tumble, Martin seemed to be no worse for wear, returning to his cabin just after dark. He lit a fire and lantern, and then made a terrible discovery—the copper samples were gone.

Martin repeated this story to Jim Edwards and also to Loy Green, who was working for Martin at the time. Green explained that weather had prevented Martin from returning to the site the rest of that season. Still, Green recalled that Martin seemed optimistic. "He knew where he had been and knew that he had found his Bonanza."[255] Martin told Green about a vivid dream he had later that night. He dreamed about his trip up the mountain, where he was again "looking at the wonderful samples of copper."[256]

By summer 1951, Martin's life had changed dramatically once again. After nearly a decade, his period of solitude at Radovan Gulch came to an end. That summer he was miraculously reunited with long-lost relatives, while at the same time, the Alaska Copper Mine Corporation decided to lease his claims with an option to buy and even planned to use his camp as a staging area for exploratory work. It seemed that Martin's dreams had finally been realized—his determination and hard work had finally paid off. After twenty-two years of working his prospects, surrounded by one of the most rugged and isolated places in Nizina country, with only Augusta, Bootsie, and his birds to keep him company, Martin—the lone prospector—had hope the modern world would make his dream come true.

Business Deals and Family Reunions
1951–1969

The passenger was a man about Martin's own height, built just as solidly and with the ruddy complexion of a man who spends a good bit of time outdoors. He wore a well fitting blue business suit. He greeted Martin and asked where he came from.

~From "Brothers Reunited in Alaska After 50 Years"
Anchorage Daily Times, November 7, 1951

"I can't go, I have to lay in my winter supplies and lay out feed for the birds." Jack was not sympathetic: "To hell with that!" "To hell with you!" said Martin.

~From "The Venerable Sourdough"
Anchorage Daily Times, 1972

By summer 1951, Radovan Gulch buzzed with activity. Extensive exploration had been undergoing in the area for two seasons.[257] As quickly as Martin staked his claims along the Augusta Vein in 1948, Alaska Copper Mines, Inc. (also known as Alaska Copper Company and the Alaska Copper Corporation) leased, with an option to buy, six of them. Fueling new interest in Martin's claims was America's increasingly hostile relationship with the Soviet Union, which stimulated exploration and development by the mining industry in Alaska. Government assistance through the Defense Minerals Exploration Administration (DMEA) authorized government assistance to explore for strategic and critical minerals, such as antimony, cobalt, mercury, nickel, tin, tungsten, and copper. One of those companies under contract for DMEA was the Alaska Copper [Mines] Corporation.[258] Under the supervision of William O'Neill, the consulting engineer, the

ABOVE: An old Alaska Road Commission bulldozer hauls freight across Glacier Creek. Martin Radovan Private Collection.

Business Deals and Family Reunions

Alaska Copper Corporation's crew consisted of nine employees including a foreman, two miners, a mechanic, a diamond driller, two helpers, and a cook. The employee hired to do the prospecting was none other than seventy-year-old Martin Radovan.[259]

In order to establish a staging area and base camp, the company radically expanded Martin's Glacier Creek camp. In addition to his small cabin originally built in 1929, the company constructed three tent-frame structures (one of which was called the Radio Shack), a sauna/generator house, an outhouse, and storage shed. The Alaska Road Commission had loaned the Alaska Copper Company a Ford dump truck and a crawler-type tractor, which had been used on the Dan and Chititu Creeks roads. The company drove the vehicles up the flood plain of the Chitistone River to the Glacier Creek camp under their own power. Employees then used the tractor to bulldoze a road to the Greenstone prospect.[260] The tractor road fronted the camp to the edge of Radovan Gulch, where it presumably crossed the Radovan Gulch glacier, and then made the steep trek up to the prospect. At the base of the prospect, the company constructed a cookhouse, an office, and a bunkhouse. Collectively, the buildings made up the Greenstone Camp.[261]

Besides providing access into the gulch, the road out of Radovan's camp was wide enough to serve as an airstrip. With the airstrip in place, the Alaska Copper Corporation was able to fly all the other equipment in by air. Two Jeeps were dismantled and flown in: One was used to haul supplies and men up the steep road to the Greenstone

A jeep used by the Alaska Copper Company crosses Glacier Creek. Note the growing camp and tractor in the background. Martin Radovan Private Collection.

Business Deals and Family Reunions

An unknown prospector at work at the Greenstone upper tunnel, date unknown. Martin Radovan Private Collection.

tunnels and camp; the other was never completely reassembled. The equipment used at the tunnels consisted of a size 125 Jaeger compressor, a size 12-B Eimco mucker, and a jackhammer with vertical bar and carriage.[262] While a majority of the employees that summer worked to build camp, blaze roadways from foot-trails, and bring in a barrage of machinery, Martin and one of the helpers worked persistently on the Binocular Prospect. Their work, however, was cut short by a snowslide that made the trail up to the prospect impassable.[263] As weather grew worse, the Alaska Copper Corporation closed up camp, while Martin reclaimed status as the gulch's lone prospector.

After Augusta died in 1944, Martin believed that he was alone in the world. This must have been hard for a man raised by a large, close-knit Croatian family. Although it had been a half century since Martin left Žrnovo, he had kept ties to his home country in distinct ways. Over the years, he maintained his Catholic faith, spoke in broken English—never fully giving up his mother tongue—and most significantly, he had not yet given up his birthright to become a citizen of the United States. Highlighting Martin's connection to the Old Country is a story retold by Emily Aiken Campbell, whose parents were one-time McCarthy residents and friends with Martin. Campbell explained that once a man walked into her family's store in Cordova speaking a language she had never heard before. Martin, who overheard, and more importantly understood, the man, "burst into tears of joy." The two men conversed well into the evening, exchanging stories in Croatian.[264]

Business Deals and Family Reunions

When Emily Aiken Campbell was a child her family ran a grocery store in Cordova. She recalled that, once while visiting her family, Martin caught a glimpse of a fruit packing label donning a picture that captured his mother's image. According to Emily, the image stunned Martin, for he had not seen his mother since 1900. Little did he know that his long-lost brother, Jack Radovich, had started a fruit packing company in Delano, California, under the brand name, "Mother." The label, as shown, displayed the image resembling their mother, Jaka. Courtesy of Aric Morton.

During World War II, Martin had lost track of his Croatian family, some of whom were still living in Yugoslavia when the Nazis invaded in 1941. After the Allied victory, mail service to Yugoslavia resumed, giving Martin hope that he might locate his remaining family. It was after Augusta's death when Martin sent them a letter. He stuck a $20 bill in an envelope and mailed it to Croatia. His sister, who had survived the war, wrote back to Martin, informing him that his brother and sister were alive and residing in Delano, California.[265] She then forwarded the letter to Martin's younger brother, Jakov "Jack" Radovanovich, who had no idea of his older brother's whereabouts.

When Martin had worked on the CR & NW Railway, he, like so many other new immigrants, sent part of his paycheck home in order to support other family members in their travel to the United States. Martin was not the only Radovanovich to make it—just the only "Radovan." Prior to World War I, Martin's brother Jack arrived to New York. On entry into the country, however, Jack's surname was shortened to "Radovich," unlike Martin, whose name was changed to "Radovan." After working for a while on the East Coast, Jack Radovich headed west. He found work in the copper mines in Arizona and later joined the military.[266] Jack served in France with the U.S. Army, and when discharged, he moved to Delano, California, where his sister lived. He started a shipping business that handled grapes and wine, and eventually, Jack's business grew into a successful vineyard. All the time, Jack never knew that his brother Martin was alive in the wilds of Alaska.[267]

Then, on a late summer day in 1951, as autumn colors transformed Radovan Gulch from green to gold, Martin noticed a small plane buzzing over camp. The Alaska Copper Corporation was gone for the season and Martin was in the process of moving from Glacier Creek to his winter cabin at Dan Creek.[268] Martin recalled that the plane landed at the Glacier Creek airstrip and the pilot and one passenger headed for camp. The passenger greeted Martin and asked where he came from:

> "They call it Yugoslavia now," Martin said. "Where are you from?"
> "I came here just now from California," replied the passenger.
> "I ought to have a brother somewhere down in California," revealed Martin.
> "What's his name?" inquired the other.
> "Jack Radovich," said Martin.
> "That's me," said the passenger and the two bothers fell in one another's arms, laughing and weeping together.[269]

Business Deals and Family Reunions

While in Anchorage, the brothers caused a bit of a stir. Martin, who had been at the gulch all summer, decided that before heading south he needed a shave and haircut. The story of the reunion found an interested audience at the 4th Avenue barber shop, and it quickly became the talk of the town. On November 7, 1951, the reunion story made front page news in the *Anchorage Daily Times*. The unexpected arrival of a rich relative prompted the *Times* article to predict, "The reunion with his brother [would end] his mining days."[270] Instead, the reunion with Jack was the start of a new mining enterprise: the Delano Mining Company.

"Brothers Reunited in Alaska After 50 Years." *Anchorage Daily Times*, November 7, 1951.

BROTHERS REUNITED IN ALASKA AFTER 50 YEARS

Meeting At Glacier Creek Brings Together Alaska Miner And California Fruit Grower

By HUGH HAMILL

Two brothers who had been separated for fifty years met recently on the banks of Glacier Creek in the Copper River country and are leaving this week for California to spend the rest of their lives together.

The brothers are Martin and Jack Radovich who parted in 1901 in what is now Yugoslavia when Martin, the younger of the two, came to America. Martin, now seventy, has worked at nearly everything during his half century in this country.

This summer he was employed by the Alaska Copper Company at its mines on Glacier Creek. Through a sister in Yugoslavia, his brother Jack learned of his whereabouts and flew to Alaska from California to meet him.

Jack has owned and operated a vineyard for the last 22 years at Delano, California, which is between Bakersfield and Fresno. Jack, who makes a comfortable profit of several thousand dollars each year from the sale of grapes, persuaded Martin to give up mining and live with him on his grape ranch in the golden state.

The brothers dropped in to Roy Nigh's barber shop on Fourth Avenue yesterday for a shave and haircut and their reunion story shortly became the marvel of the avenue.

They will fly from Anchorage to Seattle this week and then hit the air-lanes again for the jump to Bakersfield. An hour later, Martin will be exchanging happy greetings with his sister-in-law, three nieces and one nephew whom he has never seen. Martin was married for many years. His wife died in 1944.

Martin was strolling along the bank in front of his cabin at Glacier Creek Monday when he saw a plane circling overhead. The plane landed at the Glacier Creek airstrip. The pilot and one passenger headed for Martin.

The passenger was a man about Martin's own height, built just as solidly and with the ruddy complexion of a man who spends a good bit of time outdoors. He wore a well fitting blue business suit. He greeted Martin and asked where he came from.

"They call it Yugoslavia now," Martin said. "Where are you from?"

Business Deals and Family Reunions

Jack Radovich, circa 1970. Courtesy of Aric Morton.

In 1951, Martin left for California with his brother, only to return to Glacier Creek two years later. By that time, the Alaska Copper Corporation had given up its Glacier Creek options for what it determined to be better prospects in Prince William Sound. Undeterred, Martin, while in California, swayed his family to invest in his copper prospects. On May 23, 1953, Martin entered into partnership with a "Marion Radovich," (quite likely himself and backed by Jack) to form the Delano Mining Company. He then transferred the Triassic No. 30 to 32, Augusta, Boots, Ki-Ki, and Pongo Boy claims to the corporate entity. Together the claims consisted of one contiguous group of approximately four hundred acres.[271] That summer, under the auspices of the Delano Mining Company, Martin drove a drift along the Augusta Vein on the Greenstone prospect. Soon thereafter, Martin added two new claims, the "Jack," named for his younger brother, and the "Sister" claim, named for one of his wild pets.[272] By 1954, the company had one employee: Martin Radovan.[273]

The Cordova Times reported the following year that "Martin Radovan, who has been outside for several months, returned to Cordova on Saturday, and went on to his home in Glacier Creek." The paper added that a young man named Jim Edwards had also moved through Cordova, heading out to work for Radovan at Glacier Creek.[274] Edwards was actually employed by Bear Creek Mining, a subsidiary of Kennecott Corporation, which had renewed its interest in Alaska as postwar demand for minerals grew. His job was to survey the surrounding area for potential commercial sized copper deposits. Interest in Radovan's Binocular Prospect brought Edwards to Glacier Creek in 1955 and 1956. Edwards, a self-proclaimed "young buck in his twenties," first met the persistent prospector when Martin was seventy-three years old. Edwards had flown in to the Glacier Creek airstrip along with Jack Craig in February 1955.[275] The two young men disembarked the plane and followed the fresh snowshoed trail for about a mile. As they approached camp, a man greeted them with two questions: "Where are you from?" and "What can I feed you?"[276]

The Anchorage Daily Times took this photograph of Martin Radovan, but never published it with the Nov. 7 article that described Martin's reunion with his brother, Jack. Courtesy of the Alaska Daily News.

Business Deals and Family Reunions

According to Edwards, Martin treated them to "a stout meal of wild sheep meat, potatoes and freshly baked bread," and then painted for the two young men the daunting task that lay ahead. Martin explained that they would live in one of the Alaska Copper Corporation's old tent frames and work at a prospect called "Low-Contact." The following morning the work day began for the prospectors by traveling four miles on snowshoes up into a cirque, climbing a half mile in elevation on the way. The temperature for those first few weeks hovered between twenty and thirty degrees below zero, with little stoppage of high winds. With each new windstorm and snowstorm, the men were constantly forced to break new trail. Martin tried to reassure them, "Sometimes, it takes me two days to break trail." But as Edwards quickly discovered, even with the two of them taking turns, the young men still needed two days to break the trail.[277] Edwards later wrote about his work experience and friendship with Martin in an *Alaska Sportsman* article, published ten years later in 1965.

Jack Craig and Jim Edwards (second and third from the left) pose with three territorial geologists sent to assess Martin's prospects. According to Edwards, Martin spent days putting in rope and hand grips along the Binocular trail to ease their ascent. Once these geologists saw the trail to the prospect first-hand, they refused to continue on to the site. A furious Martin perceived the technocrats as simply lacking backbone. The photo was taken in front of Martin's cabin in 1955. Courtesy of Jim Edwards.

Jim Edwards (left) Martin Radovan (center) and unidentified man at Low-Contact, ca. 1965. Courtesy of Jim Edwards.

Counterclockwise: Radovan's Glacier Creek camp, ca. 1962. Courtesy of Jim Edwards.

"Drilling equipment flown in by helicopter. Snow slide was 60 degree slope" June 1967. Courtesy of Jim Edwards.

Jim Edwards and Norm Lutz at Radovan's camp, ca. 1955. Courtesy of Jim Edwards.

Drilling equipment flown in by helicopter. Snow slide was 60° slope

Working at Low-Contact, ca. 1955.
Courtesy of Jim Edwards.

Business Deals and Family Reunions

Also working for Martin that summer were Calvin and Viola Aiken. The Aikens were long-time Alaskans and had residences in both McCarthy and Cordova. Like most Copper River Valley inhabitants, the Aikens, in order to make a living, engaged in a variety of occupations. In the spring, the couple dug clams for the large razor clam canneries in Cordova. In the fall and winter, they trapped fur-bearing animals along the Bremmer River, and starting in the summer of 1955, they worked for Martin Radovan at Glacier Creek. Cal helped the men prospect for copper at Low-Contact, and Viola cooked their meals at camp.[278] Although the couple's work for Martin was brief, they formed a lasting friendship with the aging prospector. In 1960, the couple gave birth to a baby girl, Emily, and three years later, a boy named Scott. At the time, the Aikens lived in McCarthy, and wintered at their cabin in Hartney Bay in Cordova. Over the years, the Aikens began to spend less time in McCarthy to focus on their growing family and grocery store business in Cordova. As Martin aged, he began to spend his winters with them, and as Emily remembers, became a surrogate grandfather to the children.[279]

By 1955, Alaska was in the midst of change as many of its residence called for statehood. That year in Fairbanks, a group of men and women forged a constitution, blazing the trail for Alaska to become the 49th state in 1959. Martin Radovan, perhaps inspired by Alaska's statehood movement, finally decided to become a U.S. citizen. He was naturalized by the District Court of the Territory of Alaska, Third Division, at Cordova, Alaska, on September

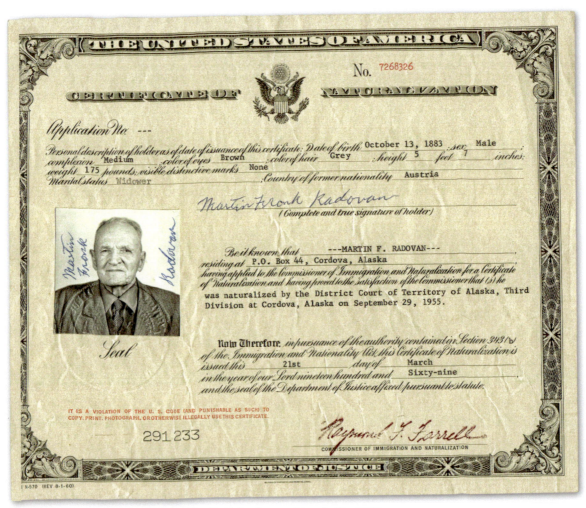

Certificate of Naturalization for Martin F. Radovan, March 21, 1969.

Calvin and Viola Aiken, worked for Martin in the 1950s.
Courtesy of Emily Aiken Campbell.

Business Deals and Family Reunions

29, 1955. Citizenship was eventually issued on March 21, 1969, when Martin was eighty-seven years old.[280] Alaska's admission into the Union did not seem to change Martin's life at Radovan Gulch, however. In 1956, the Alaska Mines Report of the Commissioner stated, "Radovan, Martin, McCarthy, Glacier Cr., Nizina Dist., McCarthy, Copper lode prospecting, 1 employed," and by 1961, two years after statehood, the Alaska Department of Natural Resources reported exactly the same thing.[281]

Between 1956 and 1962, Martin was the Delano Company's sole employee. Martin was growing older, and it was becoming more difficult for him to negotiate the gulch's treacherous landscape. In a forlorn letter to family, he noted that he worked hard during the summer of '62 and '63. He wrote that he "camped on the glacier, worked at night and slept in the day time."[282] He also expressed that life in those days was pretty lonely. "In one year I talked to just one man," he wrote, adding that it was a pilot and he had just happened to be there when he landed his plane. Perhaps because of his solitude, by the mid-1960s, Martin began to spend more and more time in California with Jack. It was probably at the urging of a worried younger brother that Martin met Wayne Thomas, Harry B. Cannon, Sr., and Frances E. Cannon and his wife, all of Tampa, Florida, and likely friends or business associates of Jack Radovich.

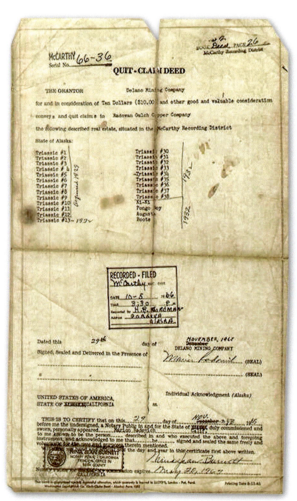

Quit Claim Deed, Delano Mining Company, November 1965.

On November 27, 1963, Martin entered into a three-party agreement with Thomas and the Cannons. A year later, on January 15, 1964, the Floridians incorporated the Radovan Gulch Copper Company and acquired title to twenty six of Martin's contiguous claims known as the Triassic Lode Group.[283] On January 9, 1964, Martin sent his California relatives a letter, describing a meeting at Radovan Gulch that changed his life:

I have a mark on my calendar November 27, 1963, a big day. A man came from Lakeland Florida to take me to Golcana [Gulkana] for a Thanksgiving dinner about 250 miles....He is a big man.... I recognize him. "Hello! Dick" "How are you Martin" "Oh, fine, how are you"..."This is your day Martin"....He pulled out a bunch of papers.... "Martin you sign here and I will witness it all right." Had a check in his wallet and gave it to me. $5000 bucks not hard to take....He told me that they will have a crew here as soon as weather permits. Check is endorsed by Walter B Cannon Sr. I sent the check to the Cordova Bank. They gave me credit for it. **I thank God for it.**

Under the terms of the agreement, Martin conveyed the fee simple real property to Cannon; Cannon could then mine and take all valuable ore from the earth. In return, Cannon and the Radovan Gulch Copper Company had to pay Martin $5,000 upon date of acceptance; $5,000 on June 1, 1965; and $10,000 on each of the following dates: June 1, 1966; June 1, 1967; June 1, 1968; and

Business Deals and Family Reunions

June 1, 1969.[284] By 1965, a supplemental agreement with the Radovan Gulch Copper Company added ten more Radovan Gulch claims: the Jack, Sister, and Triassic 39-46 claims.[285] With the new company and what looked like serious backing, Jim Edwards returned to Glacier Creek to work on the Low-Contact claims. Local resident Loy Green also started work at Glacier Creek as a camp cook for the exploration crew.[286] Martin, not surprisingly, was hired to conduct the assessment work for the company.

Bulldozer and helicopter at Glacier Creek in June 1967. Note Martin wearing his signature felt hat on the right side of the photograph. Courtesy of Jim Edwards.

Martin saw his role as a position of importance and respect. In 1967, he wrote his niece, Jack's daughter Katherine Cesare, telling her that the new president of the company, Mr. Pascoe, and the treasurer and stockholder, Mr. Thomas, had "great confidence" in him as a prospector, noting "all they [the company] do here is on my word, where to work and what they will find."[287] He then went on to describe the company's work in the gulch that summer: "They have 6000 feet of cable up there at the head of the gulch [Greenstone prospect], also [a] Diamond Drilling outfit. And set up a step ladder 150 feet high up where they [are] going to drill."[288]

Martin, however, was growing increasingly frustrated by the company's hired laborers, whom he felt, unlike locals such as Edwards, the Aikens and Green, were ill prepared, untrustworthy, and unsafe. In a letter to the Radovan Gulch Copper Company, Martin, in his distinctive broken English, provided the company an update of the 1969 season:

> *Gentlemen, I write to ask a few questions, if you have a time please....All men comes from Fairbanks to work here just a bunch of hoodlums never been off the sidewalk before, and getting $1400, a month. These men don't know how to take care of themselves and no one here to tell them how, then one gets hurt then no one goes up again. That is the situation today.*[289]

Martin's complaints continued. Not only did all the employees leave camp on the third of July to celebrate the holiday in town, they did not return for five days. By the time they returned, the weather had warmed and the creek water had risen, and when the aptly called greenhorns attempted to move the big bulldozer across Glacier Creek, they got it stuck. The water eventually flooded over the vehicle. "And there she stands for the summer," wrote Martin. "I could see that this Summer is gone."[290]

Still, as promised, the Radovan Gulch Copper Company had paid Martin $40,000 by 1969, and all the while, Martin continued to do the assessment work for the company.[291] Although the company held 172 claims, the company manger, E.B. Anderson, wrote Martin in August 1969, requesting that he limit his work to 91 claims. Anderson offered to give Martin 50 percent interest on those claims. They authorized him to spend $3,000 in assessment work on the 91 claims, including his original 26 claims. The action, however, caused Martin to worry that the company intended to release claims that had not yet been "clearly defined."[292]

Business Deals and Family Reunions

Martin responded with a handwritten letter admonishing Anderson and the company for not making a deal with Hana Mining Company, a local contractor who, according to the prospector, "had seven men willing to work the properties."[293] Martin, now eighty-seven years old, complained, "I am too old to take that kind of job. This is a time to be mining and shipping ore, price is up to 46-pound." Then Martin—who had made more money with this company than at any point in his life, added—"*Money is no good to me when I am dead*." What mattered most to Martin was finding the copper and validating his life's work. He concluded the letter with a bill for $173.86.[294]

In September, Anderson sent Martin's attorney a letter, reiterating the company's position. "I strongly urge you to advise Martin that we will not support any work above the $3,000 authorized," wrote Anderson, adding that the company will not "be responsible for debts incurred by Martin Radovan." Though sympathetic to Martin's quest— "if Martin desires to spend his own money on the other 81 claims, we will give him a 50% interest in them"—the company was nevertheless "willing to run the risk of letting someone else stake them [the claims] when the proper time has elapsed."[295]

Camp cook, Loy Green, later recalled, "They [Radovan Gulch Copper Company] succeeded in cleaning out the gut at a cost of $800,000 and found <u>nothing</u>....They suddenly stopped, transported everyone out and that was the END."[296] According to Green, the company granted Martin a life-time permit to live in his cabin. And although Martin had complete security and could live at Glacier Creek in the summer and winter at his choosing, the arrangement "was not fulfilling his dream." He filed a lawsuit for breach of contract, claiming the company failed to "find the discovery that Martin knew was there."[297] But the lawsuit went nowhere. Meanwhile, Radovan Gulch Copper Company voluntarily dissolved itself in 1971; and making good on his threat, Thomas sold the Glacier Creek claims to the Geneva-Pacific Corporation of Illinois.[298]

The Making of a Legend: Martin's Final Years in the Nizina Country
1970–1975

Knowledge and success is not produced from a mountain. Neither can brains be poured in to the place where they were left out.

~Martin Radovan
Martin's Dream

At age eighty-eight, Martin continued to work his claims at Radovan Gulch during the summer months. The *Fairbanks Daily News-Miner*, citing mining activities for 1970, reported that the prospector had "worked in the McCarthy area."[299] By the 1970s, however, Martin, just shy of ninety, started wintering in Cordova with his good friends, the Aikens. In family photographs, Martin appears happy as he celebrated holidays surrounded by pets and children. Emily Aiken was only a child then. She later recalled that her mother, Viola, was quite fond of Martin. One day she had helped him unpack his bags from Glacier Creek. "Suddenly, Mother started screaming," laughs Emily. "Inside one of Martin's bags was a rotting, smelly grizzly bear claw!" Reporter Dan Casley wrote about Martin's bear encounter in a human interest article for the *Anchorage Daily Times*. In the 1972 article, Martin, whom Casley described as a "venerable sourdough," displayed the big grizzly paw of the animal he shot, after it had raided his cabin.[300]

Though amusing, Emily's story speaks to darker activities Martin had witnessed at Glacier Creek in recent years. Granted, most self-respecting Alaska sourdoughs told "bear tales," but Martin killed animals only when it was necessary, done only when no option was available: "We only killed what we needed to eat here, or like the bear, where it was the only cure," explained Martin. But when he returned to Glacier Creek in the spring of 1970, Martin found all of his firewood burned, his cook shack pushed off into a creek, and shotgun shells everywhere. "Since those guys set up camp all the animals have left the gulch," complained Martin. "My birds were tame, they went to them like they came to me, and last year they were killed."[301]

ABOVE: Martin's self-portrait taken with a freshly shot bear, date unknown. Martin Radovan Private Collection.

Martin Radovan with bear claw in 1972.
Anchorage Daily Times collection,
Anchorage Daily News.

2A—Anchorage Daily Times Saturday, November 4, 1972

Venerable Sourdough Relates Alaskan Tales

By DAN CASLEY
Times Staff Writer

He didn't look like a bear hunter, the little old man in the tweed suit carrying the huge bear paw, but he said he'd killed the bear near his cabin.

He said his name was Martin F. Radovan, that he was 92, and for most of the summer the bear had been raiding his cabin on Glacier Creek in Radovan's Gulch, about 30 miles outside McCarthy.

"The bear, he finally bothered me all night one night," said Radovan. "But there was nothing I could do as it was dark, and my eyes, they're not so good anymore."

"I waited for daylight and then stepped outside with my rifle," he continued. "The bear was about 10 feet away."

"I said to that bear 'Let's settle this for all times to come, you go your way and I go mine, never to see one another again'," said Radovan. "But that bear wouldn't budge, he wouldn't move an inch to go, so I killed him."

Radovan said he had shot the bear on Sept. 6, and that he'd come to tell the story, and, besides that, he was leaving Alaska and he thought people might like to know the story of a man who had lived in one area of Alaska for over 50 years.

In his own way, and prompted by questions, Radovan told his story, the story of a true Alaskan Sourdough. As he spoke, it was evident that his mind was still sharp, even though nearly a century of living was etched in wrinkles and creases on his face.

He looks more like a man of 60 than of 92, except when he walks. Then the years betray him, as he walks in a hunched-over position, carefully placing one foot in front of the other.

Radovan's life started in a small town in Austria on Oct. 13, 1880. He lived there until he was approaching his 19th birthday.

At the age of 19 during the turn of the century in Austria, young men were drafted into the military service for four years. Radovan didn't want to serve under what he called "too strict military" so he decided to migrate to the United States, where he heard there was plenty of work.

Boarding a boat in June of 1900, Radovan steamed to New Jersey, arriving on July 1.

He began work in a pencil factory in New Jersey for $3 a week, with the promise of getting a one dollar per week raise at the end of the first year. After he had put in his year, he learned that his raise amounted to only fifty cents per week.

"When he refused to give me my proper raise, I quit and went down the road," he said.

Leaving the pencil factory, Radoman traveled east where he worked on the Erie Railroad Float Bridge, which spanned one of the rivers flowing out of Lake Erie. Radovan was foreman of the night crew building the bridge, and after an accident one night in which one of the pontoon floats that supported the spans sunk, he was put on a one-month layoff.

Deciding that he'd rather quit than not work for a month, Radovan decided to pursue advertisements he'd seen to work on the Cordova and Northwestern Railroad in Alaska. The pay was supposed to be $3 a day, much more than he'd ever made in any job.

He arrived on Oct. 9, 1908 at Cordova, and went to work on the railroad, which was being built up to Kennicott where there were many copper strikes. He worked for the railroad for four years, long enough to see it completed.

Radovan worked at a variety of positions on the railroad, and said that he had learned bridge building and some engineering there.

With the railroad completed, and mining booming,

HUNGRY AS A BEAR

This black bear was one of the moochers that Radovan fed in the spring when there was not much food about. The bears would come begging right up to the cabin door. Radovan said that he once had a bear eating out of his hand within three days.

Radovan took a job for a hydraulic mining company, Androse Mining Co. of New York. His job was on Chititu Creek, and he was mining for gold, not the copper he was to seek later.

While working for Androse, Radovan built a cabin on nearby Dan Creek, where he spent his winters when there was no mining activity. In 1911 he'd married, and his wife, Augusta, lived with him except when she worked as a postmistress in Cordova.

He had staked his own claim and he worked it until 1928, when the Kennicott strike for copper was on.

"I set out to stake my own claim up there (Kennicott), and it took all summer to make the trip," said Radovan. "That country was full of snowslides, rockslides and mudslides. A man's life wasn't worth the price of a meal for a dog."

In 1928 he made his claim on Glacier Creek, where he has lived until this year, with the exception of the past few winters spent in Cordova.

In 1914 Radovan received a patent on an invention he made that would have prevented a train accident he witnessed. Track on the railroad was laid in summer, and during the winter the steel contracted, leaving a gap between the rails. Radovan invented a plate and design for the ends of the ties that cured the problem, but it has never been used.

Radovan is a great animal lover, and the animals seem to sense it. While working on the railroad Radovan made friends with numerous black bears, and had one eating out of his hand within three days. Radovan fed bears, Canadian sparrows, and other animals during the spring when food was scarce.

His most faithful pet was a red fox named Bootsie Boy that stayed with him through several years.

"I first saw him one morning when I went down to the river to knock a hole in the ice for water," said Radovan. "I looked up to see him standing 15 feet away. He ran in a big circle, about 200 feet, and returned to the spot where he started."

"I said to him, 'Are you hungry, boy?', come with me for something to eat."

The fox followed Radovan into his cabin, where he immediately jumped up on Radovan's bed. Bootsie Boy became a member of the family, and would not go out of sight unless Radovan was with him.

With the snow level up to the roof, it was easy for the fox to walk up there. He slept close to the stovepipe, where it was warm.

"Whenever anything moved there in my valley, whether it be man or animal, Bootsie would scratch some bare boards next to my stove pipe until I came out to see what it was," said Radovan. "He was better than the best watchdog."

"Animals know when you like them, they sense it," he said. "I think more of them than I do of myself."

Radovan and his wife didn't have any children, and she died in the early 1960's. Radovan thought that he was completely without family, but circumstances were to prove otherwise.

When Radovan was working on the Cordova and Northwestern Railroad he had sent money to Austria so that his younger brother, Jack, could come to the United States. His brother came over and was working in New York just prior to World War I, and one of Radovan's sisters was living in Delano, Calif.

With the outbreak of the war, Radovan's brother left to work in the copper mines in Arizona, and shortly after arriving there he joined the military. Radovan lost track of him, and he also lost track of both of his sisters, one of whom was in Austria, where the mail could not go through.

It wasn't until after World War II that Radovan was able to get in touch with his family. He stuck a $20 bill in an envelope and mailed it to Austria, hoping to locate his family.

His sister in Austria was still alive, and she wrote to Radovan telling him that his brother Jack and his other sister were living in Delano, Calif.

Upon arriving in the United States, both Radovan and his brother had dropped three letters from their middle of their last name and added a suffix. Radovan chose the "an" suffix, and his brother chose "ich." Therefore his brother's name was Jack Radovich.

Jack then served three years in France with the U.S. Army, and when discharged he moved to Delano, where his sister lived. He started a ship-
(Continued on Page 3)

MARTIN F. RADOVAN, 92

Radovan displays the paw of the big grizzly that he shot on Sept. 6 of this year, after it had raided his cabin. Radovan said he shot the bear between the eyes at 10 feet with a 30-06.

"Venerable Sourdough Relates Alaskan Tales." *Anchorage Daily Times*, November 4, 1972.

The Making of a Legend:
Martin's Final Years in the Nizina Country

The so-called "guys" of the Radovan Gulch Copper Company sold their claims to the Geneva-Pacific Corporation, a technical management company in the natural resource field, which had obtained the rights to several properties in the Peavine/Glacier Creek area of the McCarthy Quadrangle of Radovan Gulch. As with the other companies that had worked at Glacier Creek, Geneva-Pacific's main objective was to explore for copper, not mine it. In the 1970s, Geneva-Pacific conducted research and development for its parent company, Belden Corporation. Belden started as a wire manufacturing upstart just at a time when the nation was becoming electrified at the turn of the century. With the introduction of inventions like television and computers, the 1950s and 1960s saw the company become a leader in the design and development of wire, cable, and cord products. By the early 1970s, Geneva-Pacific, Incorporated, a subsidiary of Belden, had launched a joint venture to explore for minerals used in the manufacturing of its products. Belden President Bob Hawkinson was personally optimistic about moving operations northward, boasting that "The Alaska properties could be a big plus in our future."[302]

While inspecting the company's Alaska claims in 1972, Hawkinson and Geneva-Pacific President Ted Van Zelst visited Radovan's camp on Glacier Creek. There they met "the legendary prospector, Martin Radovan," who made an impression on these men of business. Over the years, Martin interacted with many professional geologists and exploration companies, and even now Martin held doubts about industry's experts.[303] A photograph of Hawkinson and Martin taken during the visit reveals the aging prospector wearing his green plaid flannel shirt, red suspenders, and fedora, and appropriately holding a pair of binoculars, appearing old, but fit. At ninety, Martin could neither tunnel into rock nor hike up the gulch, but it is clear in the photograph that he was doing his best to show the Belden president where to drill.[304] Soon thereafter, a historical overview appeared in an issue of *Beldenews*, a monthly magazine that retold Martin's story, revealing, at least publically, what the company thought of Martin:

> *An area named the Binocular Prospect was first explored by a legendary prospector, Martin Radovan. Not until recently could these claims be reached by exploration crews. Before, the site was only examined through binoculars, hence the name of the prospect. Radovan and his wife climbed to the site in the 1930s to stake their claims which are now owned by Geneva Pacific...Radovan continued exploring the area well into his 80s. He sometimes climbed over the mountain and followed a narrow ledge only a foot wide, some 4000 feet above the valley floor. He and his wife lived alone in this wilderness area after the Kennecott Mines were closed. After his wife died in 1944, Radovan stayed in Alaska by himself, continuing his search for copper he so strongly believed was there.*[305]

Martin left a hand-written sign on his cabin door, stating: "Sept 15, 1971. Please do not bunk in my house. I will be back in a few days. Martin F. Radovan." Martin Radovan Private Collection.

Adding to Martin's "legendary" status are the numerous stories told and retold by local residents who knew him during these later years. McCarthy resident Gary Green worked for the prospector in the early 1970s. Martin's age and inability to work had forced him to hire help in keeping his claims current. Under Martin's instructions, Gary attempted to gather samples for Martin at his gold lode claim at Dan Creek. He even worked for a short time at the Binocular Prospect. According to Gary, he never found any copper, but he did discover the mattress that Martin had dragged up on the cliff in order to sleep on while he worked.[306] During this time, Martin continued to move between Dan Creek and Glacier Creek. On one such trip, he left a note on his cabin that read, "Spt. 15th 71. Please do not bunk in my house. I will be back in a few days. Martin F. Radovan."

Bledson President Bob Hawkins inspects Geneva-Pacific's holdings at Glacier Creek in 1972. Martin never stopped expressing his desire to develop the Binocular Prospect. Geneva-Pacific Collection, National Park Service.

The Making of a Legend: Martin's Final Years in the Nizina Country

Over the years, Martin kept in touch with his family in California. This letter was written in February, 1967. Martin Radovan Private Collection.

By the early 1970s, Martin had thought about leaving Alaska permanently to live with his family in California. He told Casley in 1972 that his family worried about him. "They're so convincing down there for me to stay," said Martin, again his words spoken in characteristically broken English. "I don't have to do anything there, and I travel all over with my brother."[307] In September 1974, Martin left Glacier Creek to live with the Aikens in Cordova, leaving his cabin as if he fully intended to return. But in February 1975, Martin made the hard decision to move to Delano. At the time, Martin was asked if he would ever return to Cordova. The ninety-three-year-old prospector smiled and said, "Oh, maybe, I don't know. I like to help the kids there—All the kids, like me in Cordova."[308]

Martin Radovan with three-year-old Emily Aiken in front of her family's home in McCarthy, circa 1960s. Courtesy of Emily Aiken Campbell.

The Making of a Legend:
Martin's Final Years in the Nizina Country

"Uncle" Martin lived in Cordova with the Aikens during the latter part of his life, here posing with a dressed-up Emily and brother Scott. Years of wear and damage give this circa 1973 photograph a timeless quality. Note Martin's camera bottom right. Courtesy of Emily Aiken Campbell.

Three months after Martin left Alaska, a two-man team from Geneva-Pacific reached Binocular Prospect using a helicopter. The men took about two hundred pounds of channel samples. A Geneva-Pacific news release optimistically alluded that modern methods would open up the hard-to-reach areas of Alaska, boasting that "Alaska has entered a new age where out-of-the-way areas can be reached more easily for mineral explorations."[309] The news gave Martin hope that they would discover the copper mountain he believed existed. However, before Martin received word as to what the geologists had found, on June 20, 1975, Martin Radovan died at a hospital in Delano, California.[310]

Between 1977 and 1978, the Coastal Mining Company completed drilling work at the gulch for Geneva-Pacific, but according to Van Zelst, the company "did not come up with the results of mineralization which met their expectation." Without Martin's claims producing anything of value, Geneva-Pacific decided to discontinue its work in the Glacier Creek area.[311] This decision corresponded with President Jimmy Carter's designation of all of the land surrounding the Peavine-Glacier Creek-Radovan area a National Monument, which severely restricted the exploration and potential mining activities in the area. Instead of pursuing further development, then, Van Zelst chose to donate the land to the National Park Service soon after the Wrangell-Saint Elias National Park and Preserve was created in 1980. In doing so, Van Zelst, and his new company, Cooper Industries, made the largest

The Making of a Legend: Martin's Final Years in the Nizina Country

Certificate of Death, Martin F. Radovan, June 20, 1975. Martin Radovan Private Collection.

land donation in Park Service history.[312] That same year, the company's director of public relations, Thomas Sykes, wrote an article profiling Martin's life. "It was his dream that there was a huge mountain of copper at what is now known as Radovan Gulch," wrote Sykes. "He worked a lifetime to prove it."[313]

A month after Martin's death, Phil R. Holdworth, P.E., an engineer and mining consultant, sent the Cesare family a letter describing Martin's Alaska holdings. He explained that Martin's mining claims continued to be in option

The Making of a Legend: Martin's Final Years in the Nizina Country

agreement with Geneva-Pacific, on which all payment had been completed (although Martin, on occasion, claimed that the final payment was not made.) He noted that the last assessment work the company conducted on the Augusta 1-8 Gold lode claims at Dan Creek was in 1972 and therefore had lapsed. This was also true for the placer claims at Dan Creek, Bessie Nos. 1 & 2, which had lapsed in 1959. He noted that "there was mention" that Martin owned a cabin on Dan Creek and a piece of property in the McCarthy Townsite, but he found no legal confirmation of either property. As to Martin's Glacier Creek holdings, the consultant wrote, "Having been one of the last to visit Martin at his cabin on Glacier Creek last year I do not believe there is much, if anything, of real value in that cabin."[314]

After a lifetime of work, Martin's pursuit of copper, and the things he left behind, lacked real "value." But today archeologists and historians recognize the cultural and historical value of Martin's uniquely preserved properties, for they convey to visitors a way of life in the Wrangell Mountains that has a great deal of meaning to the people who still live there. When Van Zelst donated Radovan's camp and the adjoining sites to the National Park Service, he recognized that their worth equaled a wilderness value, stating, "This property has an outstanding characteristic in that it can...be developed to substantial recreational and educational potential."[315] The camp itself contains an array of artifacts that collectively reflect a lifetime of mining activity. Martin's prospects and camp reflect how later capitalized corporations, such as the Alaska Copper Company, Delano Mining Company, Radovan Gulch Mining Company, and the Geneva-Pacific Corporation, influenced his independent prospecting lifeway in his twilight years. The sites reflect a period of extensive expansion and development, most demonstrated by the arrival of modern power machinery (bulldozers, jeeps, snow machines, compressors, and rock drills, for example) that significantly changed the ways in which prospecting was undertaken in the gulch. Despite this, there is evidence that Martin himself continued to prospect by hand in parallel with the more intensive operations of the companies leasing his claims. By the early 1970s, Martin, in his early nineties, was still living in Radovan Camp seasonally and attempting to attract outside interest in his mining claims. As autonomous as Martin was as a prospector, he was dependent upon outside interest for most of his mining career. Indeed, for those who knew him, Martin's real value was his larger-than-life, legendary story. As a National Park Service archeologist who visited the site wrote:

> *One cannot help but feel the presence of Radovan, perhaps as a young man laying in the single room long cabin on his grizzly bear skin and dreaming of riches yet to be fulfilled. Nor can one easily miss his presence as an old story-teller waiting in the "main house" for any available ear to come by to spin tales and weave yarns about the treasures of Radovan Gulch—dreams which in reality only existed in his mind's eye.*[316]

In the end, it is the Binocular Prospect, and its incredible story, that represents Martin's courage, his ingenuity, and his position as the "little guy." It shows how Martin pitted himself against one of the most financially successful operators in Alaska history. Perhaps sensing the large company's expansion needs, Martin managed in a week without any outside help beside his wife to reach the contact and stake thirty claims. In doing so, he beat the Kennecott corporation, took a substantial amount of the contact for himself, and secured himself a place as a significant figure in local history. Likewise, the Low-Contact property reflects Martin's famed persistence and tenacity, and how he embedded himself in a dangerous and perilous natural landscape. Martin hiked to the head of the gulch day and after day, acquiring a vast knowledge about the area through extremely hard work. Nevertheless, Martin's local knowledge of the area paled in comparison to the expertise of the professional mining engineers who eventually dominated the decision-making on which Martin was completely reliant. In his forty-five years at Radovan Gulch, Martin personally experienced significant changes in Alaska's mining industry, including the mechanization and industrialization of the technology used by miners, as well as the narrowing of expertise and the increasing professionalization of mining activities that eventually marginalized Martin's more pragmatic prospecting skills.

"Radovan Tent Frame at Glacier Creek." Sketch by Nicole Mikesh, National Park Service, 2007.

The Making of a Legend:
Martin's Final Years in the Nizina Country

View of the upper camp from the Greenstone prospect. Below is the Radovan Glacier, Glacier Creek, and Martin's original Glacier Creek campsite. Geneva-Pacific Collection, National Park Service.

A year after Martin died, a sampling team for Geneva-Pacific reported that they were stunned to discover, at 7,000 feet, a rock hammer, pick-ax, and copper ore samples hidden in a crevice by Martin Radovan. Despite forty-seven years of weathering and mineralization, the hand-made hammer and ax remained in "a remarkably good state of preservation."[317] In the end, Van Zelst recognized that the legend of Martin Radovan left a resounding mark, reminding Martin's surviving relatives that "The glacier in the gulch is called the Radovan Glacier." Loy Green agreed with Martin's legendary status. "I should mention," affirmed Green, "that the canyon he lived in was and is officially named Radovan Gulch!"[318] Considering his propensity to remain anonymous all those years, Martin Radovan, through his determination and persistence, made a name for himself—a name that no Alaskan, once hearing his incredible story, could ever forget.

Tunnel Vision:
A Prospector's Legacy

Lay on your back, relax, place palms of your hands over your eyes...Press down on your eye ball lightly, then you will see and hear everything inside of yourself. You will see your tomorrow and yesterday.

~Martin Radovan
Martin's Dream

On June 24, 1975, *The Delano Record* published Martin Radovan's obituary, reducing his life's pursuit to one sentence: "Radovan was a mining prospector in Alaska."[319] Although Martin was a simple man, his legacy in the Nizina district is far more complicated than his obituary implied. Like his hammer and pick-ax, the story of Martin Radovan's life, reflected in the properties he left behind in the Nizina Mining District, remain in "a remarkably good state of preservation." The Binocular story has inspired numerous popular articles chronicling Martin's life at Glacier Creek. In addition, every USGS report of Glacier Creek since 1931 has placed the site and trail, as well as his camp, on all official maps. Each geologist sent to survey the area has retold the story of the Binocular Prospect and has perpetuated it in the collective imagination.

As impossible as Martin's feat was, it is important to remember that Martin did not accomplish the extraordinary alone—he had Augusta. Augusta not only helped Martin build the steep trail to the Binocular Prospect, which brought him local recognition, but it was her professional skills and steady income that allowed Martin to spend his time prospecting at Dan and Glacier Creeks. While Martin remained steadfast in working his surrounding claims, Augusta interacted with the larger community of miners and their wives. Augusta fished, baked bread, sluiced for gold, cut wood, called on neighbors and friends, traveled to town usually on foot, scheduled daily life around the mail, and had a naturalist's eye for wildlife. Besides working at Kennecott from time to time, she supplemented their earnings by running the Blackburn Roadhouse with

ABOVE: **Remains of Radovan's Cabin in 2007.** Photograph by Samson Ferreira. National Park Service.

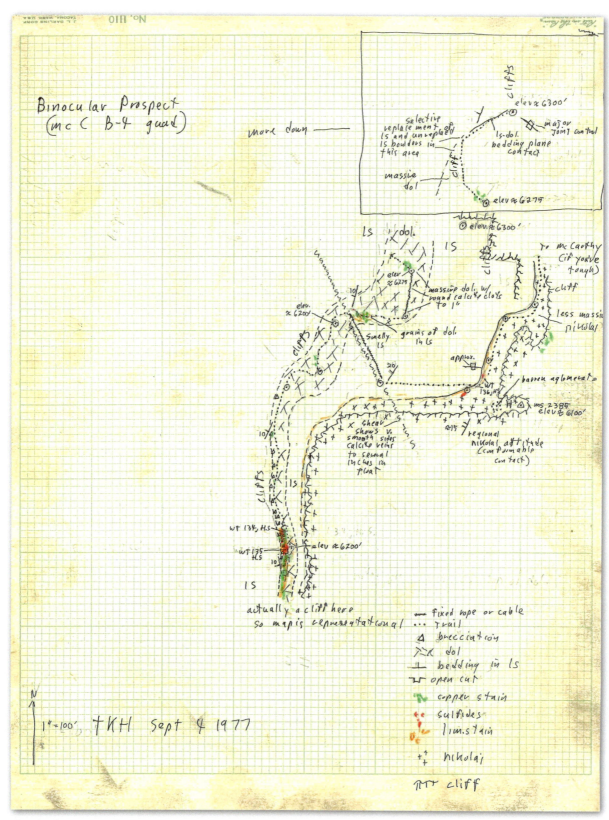

Geologic sketch of the Binocular Prospect, September 4, 1977. Geneva-Pacific Collections, National Park Service.

Tunnel Vision:
A Prospector's Legacy

Geneva Pacific geologists take samples at Binocular in 1977 or 1978. Instead of using Martin's historic trail, they reached the prospect by helicopter. Geneva-Pacific Collections, National Park Service.

Martin during the Chisana gold rush, washing miners' laundry, and assisting as the local postmistress and notary. While making a small income, she still managed to send money to her mother in Seattle. Martin also took part-time jobs when money ran short, but his aim was to find his bonanza. Although their daily work routine presented the couple usually with gender-specific, specialized tasks, Martin and Augusta shared a common vision. She not only made his dream possible, she believed in it, too.

Recent scholars of the American West have given us a framework in which to better understand the role of women in places perceived to be occupied mostly by men.[320] The scholarship draws upon methodologies from western history and women's history, and it suggests that a contradiction exists between idealized expectations of the past and the daily reality experienced by both women and men living on the frontier. This dual focus, therefore, has provided us with new ways to achieve a more complete historical understanding of the lives of women *and* men in frontier Alaska. By applying such an approach to the Radovans, Augusta's experience thus moves from the margins of Martin's story to a more central position in the historical narrative. Through Augusta's story, then, we

Tunnel Vision:
A Prospector's Legacy

and Lime stone,contact by noon,this is about a six thousand feet altitude,from here I follow,this for about a mile or so,a few bad places,but not to bad. I came to anarrpuw point,face to face,with binocular prospect,about three hundred feet from me,and about,four hundred feet higher up,it looks bad. for twenty six days,I worked hard,from twelve to sixteen hours a day,I carved out some steps, and some trail work. Always on my knee, hard going and slow work, but that,invisible hand,reaching out from the past,pushing us out to meet our environment,and guiding us in the start of our journey whispering into our ears,fear not! "The Kingdom of God is within you."go on! Made it leveled a small place to sit down.As I paused, filled with delight, at the idea,that on both side of me,my eyes rested on virgin rock never exposed to the gaze of man since,the erth began spinning round the sun. My friends thats;someahhaggtoo think about. The feeling in my heart was more then I can express in words.Mountains rear to heaven their bald and blackened cliffs, true ice and snow and bow their heads,to the Glacier below. Filld with such reflections as these, I climbed yet higher towards the top of the skypiercing peak, near the apex of which I stood, for the dawn was not far distant,and I must be on the highest stone to greet the sun when he comes,asthe,first.glance.of light from behind his shield stole through the dark abyss,of night, I threw myself prone in the summit snow,where I must remain until the,God of light was entirely victorious over the dark night.Triumphant at last! Then I arose and, making a final profound obeisance,retraced my steps down that fearful declivity of ice,and snow,and barren rock,the latter black and cruelly sharp,thrusting its ridges,through the icy coat, showing the ribs of the mountain which stood,alone to welcome me. One of the peerless peaks, of the globe,nearly ten-

"Martin's Dream." Martin tapped out his account of life in Alaska on an old typewriter, probably while living with the Aikens in Cordova during the last years of his life. When Martin died, he was buried next to his brother Jack at a cemetery in Delano, California. Martin Radovan Private Collection.

Tunnel Vision:
A Prospector's Legacy

discover that the Nizina district was inhabited by a host of extraordinary women. Some climbed mountains, some participated in national movements, most transformed communities, and many, like Augusta, came to Alaska for their own desires and dreams.

Martin came to Alaska for railroad work and stayed for gold and copper. His sixty-six years in the Nizina Mining District, nearly all spent alone or shared only with his wife, appears to fit a nostalgic, frontier image of "rugged individuals," but it is important to remember that the Radovans never acted independently from the architects of Americanization—big business and the federal government. Though they lived seemingly isolated lives in their wilderness home, they consumed processed canned foods prepared by an industrial network that connected Radovan Gulch to distant markets. Martin used Gillette shaving cream, wallpapered his cabin, and seasoned his food with spices from around the world. The presence of newspapers, magazines, and books at his cabin shows that Martin maintained a certain interest in outside events beyond the world of mining. Both he and Augusta remained creatures of an industrialized economy, taking trains or planes to towns like Cordova, Chitina, Kennecott, Blackburn, and McCarthy, towns that replicated the material, institutional, and ideological culture of rural America. Most significantly, Martin was completely dependent upon scientists to validate his claims, technocrats to mine them, and ultimately, absentee investors for the capital and ties to international markets to develop and sell the ore. Rather than evading civilization, Martin fully participated in an industrial process that transported twentieth-century American life into the heart of Interior Alaska.

Stunned geologists found Martin's hammer tucked in a crevice near the Binocular tunnel at 7,000 feet. Geneva-Pacific Collections, National Park Service.

Still, unlike many of the "rugged individuals" who left Alaska with dashed dreams, the Radovans stayed. Even after Kennecott abandoned its mines and railway in 1938, after McCarthy deteriorated into a ghost town, and after Augusta's untimely death in 1944, Martin remained at Glacier Creek. Immersed in a perilous landscape day after day, Martin picked through tons of rock and, over time, came to know the natural environment between his creekside camp and his tunnels cut deep into the mountainside. Employing only rudimentary tools and near-obsolete technology, Martin perfected climbing, construction, and prospecting skills at Radovan Gulch that inspired awe and respect from people who knew him. During his many years working in the region, Martin not only acquired the work practices of a skilled miner and prospector, but he developed an intimate relationship with and knowledge of the surrounding environment—far more than any recreationist who might visit the National Park today.[321]

Time, however, was not on Martin's side. The rationalization and scientific professionalization of mining after World War II rendered prospectors

The majestic peaks of the Wrangell Mountains surrounding Radovan Gulch. Photograph by Samson Ferreira, National Park Service, 2007.

Tunnel Vision:
A Prospector's Legacy

Martin left his trusty felt hat on his bed at his cabin at Glacier Creek, where it remains today. Photograph by Dan Trepal, National Park Service, 2010.

with his "practical" knowledge outdated. While the modern industry was still willing to examine the old-timers' claims and prospects, it now sought the expertise of university-trained engineers and geologists to determine where and how to build mines in order to efficiently and profitably extract copper. Thus, Martin's mining experience, albeit frustrating and disappointing at times, is important because it reveals a transformation of work in the Nizina district, a process of incorporation that began to marginalize the so-called "little-guy" in the mining industry throughout Alaska.

In the end, Martin, an immigrant from Žrnovo, Croatia, came half-way around the world to Radovan Gulch because of a dream—a dream he shared with none other than Horatio Alger, who mythologized America's "rags to riches" narrative. Yet, in the seventy-four years he spent in this country, Martin never achieved his dream—he never got rich. Perhaps a more compelling question is this: Why did Martin stay at Radovan Gulch? One clue comes from McCarthy resident Gary Green, who knew Martin during his last years at Glacier Creek. "Martin was a prospector," notes Green, "and a prospector always has to believe there is something to find." Likewise, Martin's longtime friend Jim Edwards agrees, "He was a prospector; he had a prospector's head...he never gave up."

Martin truly believed that his vision of copper would translate into "the greatest bonanza of all times." Still, the vision that drove Martin for four decades at Radovan Gulch seemed to move beyond the want for riches and into religious realms. His brother Jack was rich—Martin could have easily lived a life of comfort in California. Instead, he remained at Radovan Gulch, even as the infrastructure of industry collapsed around him. His friend

Tunnel Vision:
A Prospector's Legacy

Researchers discovered a copy of "Love Does Such Things" among the items Martin left in his cabin. The prospector highlighted meaningful passages that to him expressed the spirit of nature. Photograph by the author, 2010.

Jim Edwards implied that over the years the towering, ornate, circular cliffs of Radovan Gulch became Martin's wilderness cathedral, confiding that in hard times the sanctity of Glacier Creek brought him comfort—a place Jim called his outdoor "church." As he and Augusta carved the trail to Binocular, Martin later revealed that the work was "hard going and slow," but he felt that an "invisible hand, reaching out from the past, pushed us out to meet our environment, and guiding us in the start of our journey whispering into our ears, 'Fear not! The Kingdom of God is within you, go on!'"[322]

Even when the institutions of government and business gave up on the prospector, Martin nevertheless maintained an unwavering belief that a massive "copper mountain" lay deep in the limestone. Like a Biblical knight, Martin's search for a bonanza-like discovery at Radovan Gulch became his Holy Grail. Late in life, probably during his last years in Cordova, Martin sat at a typewriter and tapped out an untitled polemic about why he left Croatia, and how he came to Alaska; most importantly, he described in passionate language the mountain that came to him in a dream. Possibly, he was writing his own eulogy, or perhaps he was reaching out to the Catholic up-bringing of his Croatian youth, or maybe he was filling a void left after Augusta died, but Martin's words transcended geology and history and looked to more divine explanations about the world around him.

On the morning he reached the Binocular Prospect for the first time, Martin's reminiscence is a confluence of words and metaphors, inspired by both the natural and supernatural:

Triumphant at last! Then I arose and making a final profound obeisance, retraced my steps down that fearful declivity [downward slope] of ice and snow and barren rock, the latter black and cruelly sharp, thrusting its ridges through the icy coat, showing the ribs of the mountain which stood, alone to welcome me. One of the peerless peaks of the globe, nearly ten [thousand feet] had been [my dream] to reach that frigid summit and cast myself a living offering on its lofty altar, thus to honor my God. I wondered if he had heard and noted me. If had, did He care? ...God of the mountain to aid me? ...Without knowing why, I looked, hoping in what may seem a blind fatuity, for Him to reveal a treasure of some sort. What is the metallic glint in the rock whose sharp point of my pick had lain bare to the rays of the morning sun?[323]

Thus, it is apparent that Martin's "tunnel vision," his life-time obsession, became more than a physical quest for copper. It became a search for meaning—meaning in a world that, in spite of life's failings, still gave him hope, a reason to live. And ultimately a reason to remain at Glacier Creek looking for something that, as one researcher pointed out, "existed only in his mind's eye."[324]

It is true that Martin's mining experience could be wearisome, but his time spent pursuing his dream was never wasted. Resident Loy Green pointed out that "Martin, even though disappointed that they had not found his discovery (and still insisting that it was there if they would just keep looking) was still a happy man, and blessed us with his stories and dreams." Admittedly, Martin's triumphs never produced great wealth, but for his Binocular feat Martin gained lasting fame; for his endurance and ingenuity he obtained local respect; and through his personal relationships—whether it was with his family, friends, wife, or wildlife—Martin attained constant companionship.

Tunnel Vision:
A Prospector's Legacy

Rousing his sustained belief that copper lay buried deep within the mountains was a spirituality that, like faith, inspired Martin to keep going each day.

Perhaps his long-time friend Jim Edwards in 1965 said it best: "I think of him [Martin] often as a kind and friendly man, and probably the most persistent one I ever knew. And on that basis, although he has passed the 80 year mark, I wonder if he's still up at six in the morning, shovel in hand, heading up to his cirque for a hard day's work on his tunnel in the ice?"[325] If the historic items he left behind could speak, they would in unison proclaim that both Martin and Augusta's presence remains at Glacier Creek. Indeed, it is not what he found, but rather, what now remains. History itself is the real treasure of Radovan Gulch. And for the people of the Wrangell Mountains with whom the Radovans most identify, this is ultimately a love story that continues to provide meaning, awe, and most certainly, hope to all who know it.

Post Script

Since the final writing of the manuscript, new information has recently come to our attention regarding Augusta's grave site. We now believe it is very likely that Martin returned Augusta to Radovan Gulch after she died in 1944, and buried her near the cabin they shared at Glacier Creek for fifteen years. This information came to me about the same time that the Alaska Miner's Association inducted Martin into the Alaska Mining Hall of Fame in November 2011. Attending the Anchorage event were Katherine Cesare, Martin's niece, and Aric Morton, Martin's grandnephew, both from California. This was the first time I had had the opportunity to meet the Radovan family since this project began a year-and-a-half ago. During our brief meeting that night, Katherine, who is a dead ringer for her Uncle Martin, shared with me this final story.

After Martin left Alaska permanently Katherine became his primary caregiver. She recalled that on a spring day in 1975, she had entered Martin's sun-filled hospital room for his daily visit and her Uncle, while seemingly gazing out the window looking at something far-off indeed, was grinning ear to ear. "What are you smiling at, Uncle Martin?" she asked. "Augusta," he replied. "Augusta is waving to me from the other side of the river."

Katherine Cesare. Photograph by the author.

A few weeks later, Martin died. The family buried Martin in a Delano cemetery next to his beloved brother Jack. For a young man who left home so long ago, who never forgot his Croatian roots, or his family ties, the eternal reunion seems fitting. But it's also somehow reassuring to believe that a part of Martin's spirit is at Radovan Gulch, among the ruins of his little Glacier Creek cabin, with his pet fox Bootsy, and his unexpected yet devoted Gussie, building trails up cliffs, towards the mountain of his dreams.

~Katherine J. Ringsmuth

Afterword

I FIRST HEARD OF MARTIN RADOVAN IN JUNE 1986, almost as soon as I first arrived in the Nizina River Valley. He had been gone for 10 years by then, but it was hard to tell that by the way people spoke of him. He was a presence—a dreamer, a crazy old prospector, a man who talked with the animals; his life was centered on the search for wealth and copper as a means to achieve it. If half the stories I heard about him were true, he was amazing. Martin is an icon of his age, a human symbol of the early years of the century when the Kennecott mines ran and provided a reason to continue searching for new copper deposits. He is also a relic, an anachronism, a throwback to earlier days when the self-taught prospector was as important to the mining industries in Alaska as the technically trained mining engineer or geologist. Martin was a remnant of the wave of hopeful treasure seekers that washed over Alaska in the wake of the great gold rushes and then receded leaving only a few like him to continue the search. Martin's life is a bridge. At one end he is the immigrant looking to better his lot, the laborer not afraid to work, the prospector looking for his fortune, the man who matured while the mines worked and money was at hand. The other end is firmly in the engineer's world. More and more, machines do the heavy lifting. While the prospector and his finds are still welcomed by mining companies, the attitudes and exploration techniques they bring to his world are different, almost alien. All his life Martin searched for the rich find. Mining companies were increasingly happier with the mountains of low-grade ore that could be processed for pennies on the pound. Quantity replaced quality in the assessment of a prospect.

Augusta was Martin's anchor for many years and a force unto herself. She supported him in his efforts financially and emotionally. She climbed the cliffs of the Binocular Prospect with him and by all accounts shared his dream. After her death, Martin kept her close, tended her grave, and kept her memory alive in the names he gave his mining claims. Together, they are part of a myth and a reality unique to the Nizina River Country and common to the North American West.

I am forever happy I heard of Martin Radovan and heard the stories, fanciful and otherwise. I am pleased Katie Ringsmuth dug so deeply into his life; brought Augusta into the recognition she deserves; and made it possible for us to walk the bridge with Martin and Augusta.

~Logan Hovis, Historian
National Park Service

ABOVE: Martin in front of his Glacier Creek cabin in 1972. Martin Radovan Private Collection.

Martin Radovan's notebook.
Martin Radovan Private Collection.

Martin Radovan Private Collection. Chico, California.

Radovan, Martin. "Martin's Dream." unpublished work, circa 1974.

Archival Collections

Chititu Mines Co Records. Archives and Special Collections, Consortium Library, University of Alaska Anchorage.

"Guide to the Metropolitan Business College Records, 1919-1981." Museum of History and Industry, Seattle, Washington.

Kennecott Copper Corporation Collection. National Park Service, Anchorage, Alaska.

National Park Service Documents

Bleakley, Geoffrey. "Selected Residents of and Visitors to the Wrangell-St. Elias Mountain Region, 1796-1950," National Park Service, May 2006.

_____. "In the Shadow of Kennecott: The Forgotten Mining Camps of the Wrangell Mountain Region." Wrangell-Saint Elias National Park and Preserve, date unknown.

Ferriera, Samson. *National Park Service Cultural Landscape Inventory: Radovan Camp*, Wrangell-St. Elias National Park and Preserve, 2009.

Grauman, Melody Webb. "Big Business in Alaska: The Kennecott Mines, 1898-1938," National Park Service, 1977.

Works Cited

Langdon, Steve, and Dave Dodson. "Radovan's Camp." Site Inventory Form, National Park Service, 1994.

Spude, Robert, Dan Taylor, and Michael Lappen. "Historic Structures Inventory in Wrangell-St. Elias National Park and Preserve," 1984.

Department of the Interior News Release, "Cooper Industries Donation in Alaska is largest in Park Service History," June 1, 1983.

Government Documents

Alaska Department of Natural Resources. Mines Report of the Division, 1961.

Brooks, Alfred H. "The Mining Industry in 1910," U.S. Geological Survey, Bulletin 480 (Washington, D.C., 1911), 23.

Dickerson, Ora B. *120 Years of Alaska Postmasters, 1867-1987.* Scotts, Michigan: Carl J. Cammarata, 1989.

Fay, Albert H. *Glossary of Mining and Mineral Industry.* Bureau of Mines, U.S. Department of the Interior, 1920.

Jasper, W. M. "Alaska, Mines, Report of the Commissioner," 13 July 1954.

Miller, Don J. "Copper Deposits of the Nizina District, Alaska." *Mineral Resources of Alaska, 1943 and 1944*, U.S. Geological Survey, Bulletin 947 F 114-117, Washington, D.C., 1946.

Moffit, Fred H., and Stephen R. Capps. "Geology and Mineral Resources of the Nizina District, Alaska." U.S. Geological Survey, Bulletin 448, Washington, D.C., 1911.

Pilgrim, E. R. "Mining investigations and mining inspection in Alaska, biennium ending March 31, 1933." *Report of Alaska Supervising Mining Engineer*, Alaska Territorial Department of Mines. 1933.

Sainsbury, C. L. *Geology of the Nelson and Radovan Copper Prospects, Glacier Creek, Alaska*. U.S. Geological Survey, 1951.

Saunders, Robert H. "Report on the Prospecting Program of the Alaska Copper Company on Claire Creek, Copper River Region, Alaska," To Associate Mining Engineer, Leo H. Saarela, Commissioner of Mines. Juneau, Alaska, Department of Mines, Territory of Alaska, 3 March, 1952.

_____. "Report on the prospecting of the Alaska Copper Company on Glacier Creek, Copper River region, Alaska," Alaska Department of Mines, 1952.

Stewart, B. D. Mining Investigations and Mine Inspection in Alaska, Biennium ending March 31, 1933, "Report on Cooperative Mining Investigations." Alaska Territorial Department of Mines, 1933.

Ransome, Alfred L., and William H. Kerns. *Mineral Yearbook Area Report.* U.S. Bureau of Mines, Vol. III, 1952.

Smith, Philip S. "Mineral Industry of Alaska in 1931 and Administrative Report." U.S. Geological Survey, Bulletin 844-A, Washington, D.C., 1933.

Works Cited

Smith, Philip S. "Mineral Industry of Alaska in 1938." U.S. Geological Survey, Bulletin 917-A, Washington, D.C., 1939.

U.S. Stat., vol. 35, chapter 269 [1909], sec. 2/pp. 839-840.

Winkler, Gary, et al. "A Geologic Guide to Wrangell-Saint Elias National Park and Preserve, Alaska: A Tectonic Collage of Northbound Terranes." U.S. Geological Survey, Professional Paper 1616, Washington, D.C., 2000.

Wright, W. S., and A. W. Tolonen. "Chitistone Copper Deposits, Chitistone River Area, Alaska." U.S. Bureau of Mines, 1945.

Books

Armitage, Sue, and Elizabeth Jameson, ed. *The Women's West.* Norman, Oklahoma: Oklahoma Press, 1987.

Dahlie, Jorgen. *A Social History of Scandinavian Immigration, Washington State, 1895-1910.* New York: Arno Press, 1980.

Dorrance, H. William, and Francis S. Morgan. *Sugar Islands: The 165-year Story of Sugar in Hawai'i.* Honolulu: Mutual Publishing, 2000.

Dunlap, Thomas R. *Faith in Nature: Environmentalism as Religious Quest.* Seattle: University of Washington Press, 2004.

Goetzmann, William H. *Exploration and Empire: The Explorer and the Scientist in the Winning of the American West.* New York: History Book Club, 1966.

Greipsland, Torbjorn. *Forgotten Norwegians in Hawaii: From Life in Slavery to Life in a Vacation Paradise.* Emigrantforlaget, 2004.

Hunt, William. *Mountain Wilderness: An Illustrated History of Wrangell-St. Elias National Park and Preserve, Alaska.* Anchorage: Alaska Natural History Association, 1996.

Kirchhoff, M. J. *Historic McCarthy: The Town that Copper Built.* Juneau: Alaska Cedar Press, 1993.

LeCain, Timothy J. *Mass Destruction: The Men and Giant Mines that Wired America and Scarred the Planet.* New Brunswick, New Jersey: Rutgers University Press, 2009.

Morse, Kathryn. *The Nature of Gold: An Environmental History of the Klondike Gold Rush.* Seattle: University of Washington Press, 2003.

Movius, Phyllis Demuth. *A Place of Belonging: Five Founding Women of Fairbanks, Alaska.* Fairbanks: University of Alaska Press, 2009.

Rasmussen, Janet E. *New Land, New Lives: Scandinavian Immigrants to the Pacific Northwest.* Seattle: University of Washington Press, 1993.

Works Cited

Robbins, William. *Colony and Empire: The Capitalist Transformation of the American West.* Lawrence: University Press of Kansas, 1994.

Sherwood, Morgan B. *Exploration of Alaska, 1865-1900.* Fairbanks: University of Alaska Press, 1992.

Stein, Alan J., Paula Becker, and the HistoryLink Staff. *Alaska Yukon Pacific Exposition: A Timeline History.* Seattle: University of Washington Press, 2009.

Takaki, Ronald. *Pau Hana: Plantation Life and Labor in Hawaii: 1835-1920.* Honolulu: University of Hawaii Press, 1983.

Trachtenberg, Alan. *The Incorporation of America: Culture and Society in the Gilded Age.* New York: Hill and Wang, 1982.

Articles

Bateman, Alan M. "Notes on a Kennecott type of copper deposit, Glacier Creek, Alaska." *Economic Geology* 27, no. 3 (1932).

"Brothers Reunited in Alaska after 50 Years," *Anchorage Daily Times*, 7 November 1951.

Davis, Eleanor H. "The Norse Migration: Norwegian Labor in Hawaii." *The Hawaiian Historical Society,* (December 1962).

Casley, Dan, "Venerable Sourdough Relates Alaskan Tale," *Anchorage Daily Times*, 4 November 1972.

Cronon, William. "Kennicott Journey: the Paths Out of Town." In *Under an Open Sky: Rethinking America's Western Past*, edited by William Cronon, George Miles, Jay Gitlin. New York: W.W. Norton & Company, 1992.

Edwards, James H. "Martin Radovan." *Alaskan Sportsman*, September 1965.

Green, Loy, "Life in the Wrangell Mts. & Meetings with remarkable Men & Women from 1963," *Wrangell-Saint Elias News*, 21 April 1994.

Hovis, Logan, and Jeremy Mouat. "Miners, Engineers, and the Transformation of Work in the Western Mining Industry, 1880-1930." *Technology and Culture* (University of Chicago Press) 37, no. 3 (July 1996).

Keen, Dora. "Arctic Mountaineering by a Woman: Mount Blackburn." *Scribner's Magazine*, July-December 1912.

Reiff, Janice L. "Scandinavian Women in Seattle: Domestication and Americanization." In *Women in Pacific Northwest History: An Anthology, edited by* Karen J. Blair. Seattle: University of Washington Press, 1988.

"Seattle's Streetcar History," *Seattle Times*, 23 December 2007.

White, Richard. "'Are You an Environmentalist or Do You Work for a Living?': Work and Nature." In *Uncommon Ground: Rethinking the Human Place in Nature*, edited by William Cronon. New York: W. W. Norton & Company, 1996.

Works Cited

Smith, Kenny, "Martin Radovan Remembered," *Wrangell-St. Elias News*, November and December 2006.

Corporate Reports/Newsletters/News Releases

Geneva Pacific. "Historical Review of Glacier Creek Area," 1979.

"Geneva Pacific Reaches the Binocular Prospect," Geneva-Pacific Corp. News Release, undated.

Larimer, Tim. "Geneva Pacific: Belden's Stake in Alaska." Geneva Pacific Corp., Subsidiary of Belden Corporation, Newsletter, 1979.

Sykes, Thomas. "Prospector Martin Radovan," unpublished article, 1980.

Newspapers

The Alaska Citizen
The Alaska Weekly
The Anchorage Daily Times
Chitina Leader
Cordova Times
Delano Record
Fairbanks Daily News-Miner
McCarthy Weekly News
The Seattle Times

Interviews/Correspondence

Jack Radovich, by Katherine Cesare, date unknown.
James Edwards, by Katherine Ringsmuth and Dan Trepal, July 7, 2010
Emily Aiken Campbell, by Katherine Ringsmuth, June 18, 2010.
Interview, Gary Green, Katherine Ringsmuth and Dan Trepal, July 10, 2010.

Correspondence with Katherine Cesare, June 10, 2010
Correspondence with Aric Morton, throughout summer 2010.
Communication with Valdez Parks and Recreation, June 2010.
Correspondence with Aurora Lang, Cordova Museum Archivist, throughout summer 2010.
Correspondence with Sunny Cook, McCarthy Museum President, September 22, 2010.

Public Records

Florida Department of State Division of Corporations
The Registry of Trefoldighetskirken (Trinity Church) in Oslo

Works Cited

(Accessed via Ancestory.com)
U.S. Census Records
WWI Draft Registration Cards
Death Certificates
Naturalization Records
Marriage License
Polk Directory
Social Security Death Index

Endnotes

[1] Dora Keen, "Arctic Mountaineering by a Woman: Mount Blackburn," *Scribner's Magazine* LII, July-December 1912.
[2] Kirchhoff, *Historic McCarthy: The Town that Copper Built* (Juneau: Alaska Cedar Press, 1993), pp. 16-17.
[3] William Cronon, "Kennicott Journey: the Paths Out of Town," *Under an Open Sky: Rethinking America's Western Past* (New York: W.W. Norton % Company, 1992), pp. 28-51.
[4] Ibid.
[5] Kirchhoff, 19.
[6] Kirchhoff, 19-20.
[7] Due to a spelling error, the mining company became the Kennecott Copper Corporation, while the glacier and surrounding area named for Robert Kennicott continued to be spelled with an "i".
[8] Wrangellia, one of the most extensively displaced terranes in North America, is a composite terrane, consisting of several exotic terranes, including the Wrangell Terrane, the geological basis of the Nizina country. Scientists believe that the massive terrane migrated from subtropical latitudes to northern temperate latitudes in the eastern Pacific between the late Triassic and late Jurassic periods, drifting some 2,500 miles or more before colliding with the North American Continent by the Cretaceous period. Although composed of many different rock types, geologists identify the late Triassic flood basalts—the distinctive Nikolai Greenstone of the Wrangell Mountains—as the defining unit of Wrangellia. For more information about Wrangellia, see Winkler, *A Geological Guide to Wrangell-Saint Elias National Park and Preserve, Alaska* (U.S. Geological Survey, Professional paper 1616, 2000).
[9] Timothy J. LeCain, *Mass Destruction: The Men and Giant Mines That Wired America and Scarred the Planet* (New Brunswick: Rutgers University Press, 2009), 32.
[10] LeCain, 32-33.
[11] LeCain, 33.
[12] Ibid.
[13] Miller, 99.
[14] For further readings on the U. S. Geological Service and its role in the process of Americanization, see Alan Trachtenberg, *The Incorporation of America: Culture and Society in the Gilded Age* (New York: Hill and Wang, 1982), 20; Morgan Sherwood, *Exploration of Alaska, 1865-1900* (Fairbanks: University of Alaska Press, 1992), 172; and William Robbins, *Colony and Empire: The Capitalist Transformation of the American West* (Lawrence: University Press of Kansas, 1994), 68.

Endnotes

[15] Fred H. Moffit and Stephen R. Capps, "Geology and Mineral Resources of the Nizina District, Alaska," U.S. Geological Survey, Bulletin 448, 1911, p. 8.

[16] "Brothers Reunited in Alaska after 50 Years," *Anchorage Daily Times,* 1951.

[17] Geoffrey Bleakley, "In the Shadow of Kennecott: The Forgotten Mining Camps of the Wrangell Mountain Region," Wrangell-Saint Elias National Park and Preserve, date unknown.

[18] Steve Langdon and Dave Dodson, "Radovan Camp," Site Inventory Form, National Park Service, 1994.

[19] Marion was anglicized to Martin when he came to the United States in 1900.

[20] "Martin Radovan" World War I Draft Registration Cards, 1917-1918.

[21] Thomas Sykes, "Prospector Martin Radovan," unpublished article, written in 1980.

[22] Church Records, Zrnova, Korcula, courtesy of Katherine Cesare, 10 June 2010.

[23] Dan Casley, "Venerable Sourdough Relates Alaskan Tale," *Anchorage Daily Times,* 4 November 1972.

[24] Martin Radovan, *Martin's Dream,* unpublished, circa 1974.

[25] *Martin's Dream.*

[26] Casley, "Venerable Sourdough," 1972; NOTE: No immigration records have been located for a Martin Radovanovich passing through Ellis Island.

[27] "Brother Reunited in Alaska after 50 Years," *Anchorage Daily Times,* 7 November 1951; "Venerable Sourdough," *Anchorage Daily Times,* 4 November 1972; Geneva Pacific, "Historical Review of Glacier Creek Area," 1979.

[28] *Martin's Dream.*

[29] Casley, "Venerable Sourdough," 1972.

[30] Interview, Martin Radovan by Katherine Cesare, date unknown. Martin Radovan Private Collection, Chico, California.

[31] Ibid.

[32] Correspondence with Katherine Cesare, 10 June 2010.

[33] "Brothers Reunited in Alaska after 50 Years," *Anchorage Daily Times,* 1951.

[34] Casley, "Venerable Sourdough," 1972.

[35] Ibid.

[36] Ibid.

[37] Melody Webb Grauman, "Big Business in Alaska: The Kennecott Mines, 1898-1938," National Park Service, 1977, p. 8.

[38] Grauman, 6; Hovis

[39] Grauman,

[40] Kirchhoff, 23.

[41] Grauman, 6-7.

[42] By 1909 the Syndicate had acquired the whole Company, three thousand acres of lode and placer claims, for $2,987,500. Grauman, 7.

[43] Grauman, 9.

[44] LeCain, 27-28.

[45] LeCain, 26-27.

[46] LeCain, 31.

[47] *Martin's Dream.*

[48] Kirchhoff, 25.

[49] Alfred Brooks, "The Mining Industry in 1910," U.S. Geological Survey, Bulletin 480 (Washington, D.C., 1911), 23.

[50] *Martin's Dream.*

[51] "Brothers Reunited," 1951; Casley, "Venerable Sourdough," 1972.

[52] Casley, "Venerable Sourdough," 1972.

[53] "Martin E. Radovan," U.S. "Brothers Reunited in Alaska after 50 Years," *Anchorage Daily Times,* 1951 Census Records, 1910; NOTE: The census record states that Martin immigrated in 1878, several years before he was born. There is a good chance the recorder wrote a seven instead of a nine and Martin actually immigrated to the U.S. around 1898. This would be closer to Martin's date 1900, which he gives in *Martin's Dream.*

[54] "Martin Radovan" WWI Draft Registration Card.

[55] "Martin Radovan," U.S. Census Records, 1920.

[56] NOTE: According to Martin's friend and employee, James Edwards, Martin did not like having his picture taken. Thus, his efforts to remain anonymous may, at least in part, explain why historians have found so few photographs of Martin as a young man.

Endnotes

[57] The spelling of the Iversen family changed to" Iverson" after the family reached Seattle, Washington.

[58] The Registry of Trefoldighetskirken (Trinity Church) in Oslo. NOTE: Norwegian census and church records were provided by Kate Nordby, a Norwegian genealogy researcher.

[59] NOTE: Local newspapers in Drammen, Tidende, and other towns throughout Norway printed the following message with hopes of attracting hard-working help: "Contracts with those who will go to the Sandwich Islands, are drawn up and signed on Wednesday, Sept 23, and the following days at the office of Hans P. Faye, at Drammen from 11 to 3 o'clock. The parties must be provided with good recommendations, and attestations for good and faultless behavior. Parties under obligation of military service, must bring release from service. Signature for minors must, to be valid, be confirmed by guardian. The conditions are now regulated, and thus fixed: Laborers over 20 years, 9 dollars; under 20 years, somewhat less, per month, with free board, or board-money and free lodging, families may bring two children with them. Free passage and board, which is not to be worked out afterwards." Char. L'Orange, Agent of the Hawaiian Bureau of Immigration, Sandwich Islands. From Torbjorn Greipsland, *Forgotten Norwegians in Hawaii: From Life in Slavery to Life in a Vacation Paradise* (Emigrantforlaget, 2004), 4.

[60] Torbjorn Greipsland, *Forgotten Norwegians in Hawaii: From Life in Slavery to Life in a Vacation Paradise* (Emigrantforlaget, 2004), 4.

[61] The passenger lists a "Johan A. Iversen, wife, and 9 month old child" (though Augusta would have been 1 year by the date of departure.) "Passenger List for the Bark Beta." In Greipsland, 80-86.

[62] Eleanor H. Davis, "The Norse Migration: Norwegian Labor in Hawaii," *The Hawaiian Historical Society Seventy-First Annual Report*, December 1962, 28-35; "Nils Emil Aars Diary," reprinted in Greipsland, 13-24.

[63] Ronald Takaki, *Pau Hana: Plantation Life and Labor in Hawaii, 1835-1920* (Honolulu: University of Hawaii Press, 1983), 41.

[64] Davis, 28-35.

[65] Quoted in *Pau Hana*, 41.

[66] William H. Dorrance and Francis S. Morgan, *Sugar Islands: The 165-year Story of Sugar in Hawai'i* (Honolulu: Mutual Publishing, 2000), 63.

[67] "Charles John Iverson," U.S. Census Records, 1920; "Charles J. Iverson," Death Certificate, King County Department of Public Health, Bureau of Vital Statistics.

[68] Davis, 28-35.

[69] NOTE: Augusta Radovan's death certificate states that she was born in Oslo, Norway, on October 23, 1884. The information was undoubtedly provided by Martin, who may not have known for sure where Augusta was born.

[70] Janice L. Reiff, "Scandinavian Women in Seattle: Domestication and Americanization," in *Women in Pacific Northwest History: An Anthology,* ed. Karen J. Blair (Seattle: University of Washington Press, 1988), 170-184.

[71] NOTE: By this point the family is spelling their surname "Iverson" rather than "Iversen."

[72] NOTE: Augusta's age calculation is based on Norwegian birth records.

[73] NOTE: In 1899 Augusta's address is "dom 216 Lenora"; Charles's address is "Acme Bus Coll, res 2910 1st av." In 1890, Augusta's address is "Wilson's MBC, beds 216 Lenora"; Charles is "1711 2d av." Thora is listed at the same address. *Polk Directory*, 1899 and 1900.

[74] NOTE: The school was originally called the Seattle Business College, but it was bought out by the Acme Business College in 1894. "Guide to the Metropolitan Business College Records, 1919-1981," Museum of History and Industry, Seattle, Washington; *Polk Directory*, 1899 and 1900.

[75] *Polk's Seattle Directory*, 1899 and 1900.

[76] "Thora Iverson" U.S. Census Records, 1900; *Polk's Seattle Directory*, 1899 and 1900; "Augusta Iverson," U.S. Census Records, 1900.

[77] "Seattle's Streetcar History," *The Seattle Times*, 23 December 2007.

[78] NOTE: For more information on Scandinavians in the Pacific Northwest, see Jorgen Dahlie, *A Social History of Scandinavian Immigration, Washington State, 1895-1910* (New York: Arno Press, 1980); Janet E. Rasmussen, *New Land, New Lives: Scandinavian Immigrants to the Pacific Northwest*, (Seattle: University of Washington Press, 1993); and Janice L. Reiff, "Scandinavian Women in Seattle: Domestication and Americanization," in *Women in Pacific Northwest History: An Anthology,* ed. Karen J. Blair (Seattle: University of Washington Press, 1988).

[79] "Augusta Iverson," U.S. Census Records, 1910.

[80] Ibid.

[81] Alan J. Stein, Paula Becker, and the HistoryLink Staff, *Alaska Yukon Pacific Exposition: A Timeline History* (Seattle: University of Washington Press, 2009).

Endnotes

[82] NOTE: The infamous Ballinger-Pinchot Affair would effectively split the Republican Party, and pit conservationists against preservationists in a battle over management of America's natural resources for decades to come.

[83] Grauman, 8-14.

[84] Ibid.

[85] Casley, "Venerable Sourdough," 1972.

[86] Winkler, "A Geological Guide to Wrangell-Saint Elias National Park and Preserve, Alaska: A Tectonic Collage of Northbound Terranes."

[87] Moffit (1911).

[88] "Brothers Reunited," 1951.

[89] Kirchhoff, 28.

[90] Kirchhoff, 29-30

[91] Ibid, 31.

[92] *Chitina Leader*, 15 July 1911.

[93] Interview, Gary Green, 10 July 2010; Kirchhoff, 34.

[94] Ibid.

[95] NOTE: McCarthy resident Gary Green, who worked for Martin in the early 1970s, remembers a story Martin told him of the Blackburn ascent. Martin had told Gary that he helped by hauling food and other supplies for the first attempt that later failed. It is unclear if he was associated with the successful 1912 ascent. Interview, 10 July 2010.

[96] Dora Keen, "Arctic Mountaineering by a Woman: Mount Blackburn," *Scribner's Magazine* LII, July-December 1912.

[97] Kirchhoff, 41.

[98] NOTE: McCarthy resident Loy Green told the *Wrangell-Saint Elias News* that Martin "married one of the secretaries from Kennecott and brought her to his cabin at Glacier Creek." Loy Green, "Life in the Wrangell Mts. & Meetings with remarkable Men & Women from 1963," 21 April 1994, courtesy of the *Wrangell-Saint Elias News*. Other evidence that the Radovans ran the roadhouse together is a menu written in an alphabetized notebook that Augusta Radovan later used as a diary. On April 9, 1931, she wrote, "1913—when we had the restaurant in Blackburn." James Edwards also remembers that Martin ran the Blackburn Roadhouse for a short time, recalling that "a patron once ran off without paying, and Martin Radovan chased him down and got his money." Interview, 10 July 2010.

[99] NOTE: The current spelling for "Shushanna" is "Chisana."

[100] Interview, James Edwards, 7 July 2010.

[101] NOTE: Kirchhoff writes that McCarthyites seriously considered changing their town's name to Shushanna Junction. Although the railroad depot did adopt the new name, the town and post office retained the name of McCarthy. Kirchhoff, 44.

[102] Kirchhoff, 42.

[103] "Martin Radovan and Augusta Iverson," Marriage License, State of Alaska, Public Records; McCarthy resident; NOTE: Loy Green told the *Wrangell Saint Elias News* that Martin "married one of the secretaries from Kennecott and brought her to his cabin at Glacier Creek." Loy Green, "Life in the Wrangell Mts. & Meetings with Remarkable Men & Women from 1963," 21 April 1994.

[104] Interview, Gary Green, 7 July 2010.

[105] Kennecott Records detailing employees prior to 1918 are scarce. The document, "Details, Gross Month Paid to All Married Men at Kennecott, December & January, 1916-1917," in which an Radovan, M is listed, was found on the wall at the Kennicott Lodge. This lucky discovery places Martin at Kennecott, and confirms that he was, at one point, an employee.

[106] NOTE: Employee records for Kennecott begin in 1918. See Kennecott Copper Corporation Collection, National Park Service, Anchorage, Alaska.

[107] "Interview Notes," Katherine Cesare talking with her grandfather, Jack Radovich, about her uncle, Martin Radovan, Date Unknown, Martin Radovan Private Collection, Chico, California.

[108] "Martin Radovan," WWI Registration Draft Card.

[109] *McCarthy Weekly News,* 8 November 1924.

[110] Correspondence with Aurora Lang, Cordova Museum Archivist, throughout summer 2010.

[111] "Martin Radovan and Augusta Iverson," Marriage Certificate.

[112] "Frank A. Iverson," Washington State and Territorial Census, 1892; *Seattle Directory*; *Polk Directory*.

[113] Geoffrey Bleakley, "Selected Residents of and Visitors to the Wrangell-St. Elias Mountain Region, 1796-1950," National Park Service, May 2006.

Endnotes

[114] "Frank Iverson," U.S. Census Records, 1920.

[115] Rasmussen (1993); Reiff (1988).

[116] "Scandinavian Women in Seattle: Domestication and Americanization," in *Women in Pacific Northwest History: An Anthology,* ed. Karen J. Blair (Seattle: University of Washington Press, 1988); Sue Armitage and Elizabeth Jameson, *The Women's West* (Norman, Oklahoma: Oklahoma Press, 1987).

[117] U.S. Stat., vol. 35, ch. 269 [1909], sec. 2/pp. 839-840; NOTE: S.D. Charles of Cordova was appointed deputy marshal for law enforcement and M.V. Lattin was appointed the U.S. commissioner.

[118] *The Alaska Citizen*, Fairbanks, Alaska, Monday Morning, 9 March 1914, vol. v. no. 1.

[119] Interview, James Edwards, 7 July 2010.

[120] Chitina Courthouse burned in the mid-1940s.

[121] "Kennecott employee records," Kennecott Copper Corporation Collection, National Park Service, Anchorage, Alaska.

[122] "Charles John Iverson," WWI Draft Registration Card.

[123] "Charles John Iverson," U.S. Census Records, 1920.

[124] "Charles John Iverson," U.S. Census Records, 1930.

[125] "Martin Radovan," U.S. Census Records, 1920.

[126] *Fairbanks Daily News-Miner*, 29 November 1917.

[127] William Hunt, *Mountain Wilderness: An Illustrated History of Wrangell-St. Elias National Park and Preserve, Alaska* (Anchorage: Alaska Natural History Association, 1996), 66.

[128] NOTE: The Kennecott Copper Corporation was incorporated in 1915 to dilute the enormous cost of building the CR&RW Railway and to find new ventures for the capital produced by Kennecott's mines.

[129] Bleakley, "Selected Residents," 2006.

[130] From Earl Pilgrim visit in 1931, republished in B. D. Stewart, *Mining Investigations and Mine Inspection in Alaska, Biennium ending March 31, 1933*, "Report on Cooperative Mining Investigations," (Alaska Territorial Department of Mines, 1933), 93. NOTE: In 1931, Acting Territorial Mine Engineer Benjamin D. Stewart appointed Earl Pilgrim a member of his staff in charge of hardrock (lode) examinations for the Alaskan Territory. (Information from the Alaska Mining Hall of Fame.)

[131] Pilgrim, 1931.

[132] Letter: To Mrs. Catherine Cesare from Phil R. Holdsworth, P.E. 20 July 1975. NOTE: The letter lists Martin's holdings in Alaska.

[133] *McCarthy Weekly News*, 21 October 1922.

[134] *McCarthy Weekly News,* 19 September 1925.

[135] *McCarthy Weekly News,* 17 February 1923.

[136] NOTE: Martin "mushed" in from Dan Creek and returned quickly. *McCarthy Weekly News,* 31 October 1925.

[137] *McCarthy Weekly News,* 27 December 1924.

[138] NOTE: John J. Price was appointed postmaster at Dan Creek in May 1924. Ora B. Dickerson, *120 Years of Alaska Postmasters, 1867-1987* (Scotts, Michigan: Carl J. Cammarata, 1989), 28.

[139] *McCarthy Weekly News*, 27 December 1924; 21 February 1925.

[140] *McCarthy Weekly News*, 28 March 1925.

[141] *Augusta Radovan's Journal*, in Martin Radovan Private Collection, Chico, California.

[142] Ibid.

[143] Ibid.

[144] Casley, "Venerable Sourdough," 1972.

[145] *Augusta Radovan's Journal*.

[146] Rim rock is the bedrock rising to form the boundary of a placer or gravel deposit. Albert H. Fay, *Glossary of Mining and Mineral Industry* (Bureau of Mines, U.S. Department of the Interior, 1920), 571.

[147] *Augusta Radovan's Journal*.

[148] Ibid.

[149] Armitage and Jameson, 14.

[150] *Augusta Radovan's Journal*.

[151] *Augusta Radovan's Journal*; NOTE: Louis Anderton came to the region in 1922, when he was hired to complete the tunnel connecting the Erie and Jumbo Mines at Kennecott. He eventually moved to the Nizina district, where he worked for the Chititu Mining Company in 1926. During the late 1930s, he prospected on Rex Creek, where he was badly injured in a mining accident. (Bleakley, 2006)

Endnotes

[152] Phyllis Demuth Movius, *A Place of Belonging: Five Founding Women of Fairbanks, Alaska* (Fairbanks: University of Alaska Press, 2009), 17.

[153] NOTE: Mr. Walter Holmes was an early resident of May Creek. In 1936 he staked in a tributary of Copper Creek in the Nizina district. Mt. Holmes, a prominent summit just south of Rex Creek, was apparently named for him. (Bleakley, 2006.)

[154] *Augusta Radovan's Journal.*

[155] NOTE: The Harrais' would soon lose their life savings in the Great Depression. (Bleakley, 2006.)

[156] Movius, 92.

[157] Ibid, 92-93.

[158] Correspondence with Sunny Cook, McCarthy Museum President, September 22, 2010. Titles noted in Augusta's Journal.

[159] NOTE: There were five different Davises associated with the Nizina district. (Bleakley, 2006.)

[160] *Augusta Radovan's Journal.*

[161] *Martin's Notebook*, Martin Radovan Private Collection, Chico California.

[162] NOTE: John "Cap" Hubrick became one of the region's first and most famous commercial outfitters, guiding sport hunters out of McCarthy during the teens and 1920s. During the off season he published a short-lived newspaper called the *Copper Bee*, and produced superb hand-tinted panoramic photos. Hubrick died in 1930. John Hart established the first Sourdough Roadhouse in 1903. (Bleakley, 2006)

[163] NOTE: Jim Murie participated in the Chisana rush. In 1916 he and his wife Tess began operating the Nizina Roadhouse. After Jim died in 1940, Tess marred her old friend Walter Holmes. (Bleakley, 2006)

[164] *Augusta Radovan's Journal.*

[165] Ibid.

[166] NOTE: Augusta's journal entry for April 16, 1931, hints at the presence of the Alaska Road Commission. William R. Cameron worked as a foreman in Chitina in 1911 and 1912 and later worked for the Alaska Road Commission; Boldy, or perhaps Bodie, prospected at Chititu Creek; Pete Brenwick lived in McCarthy and participated in the Chisana gold rush; he made much of his winter income during the 1920s supplying cord wood to Kennecott. (Bleakley, 2006)

[167] *Augusta Radovan's Journal.*

[168] Ibid.

[169] Ibid.

[170] Ibid.

[171] Ibid.

[172] Ibid.

[173] Ibid.

[174] "Augusta Radovan," U.S. Census Records, 1929.

[175] "Brothers Reunited," 1951.

[176] Interview, Gary Green, 10 July 2010.

[177] Alan M. Bateman, "Notes on a Kennecott type of copper deposit, Glacier Creek, Alaska," *Economic Geology* 27, no. 3 (1932): 297-306.

[178] Casley, "Venerable Sourdough," 1972.

[179] Robert Spude, Dan Taylor, and Michael Lappen, "Historic Structures Inventory in Wrangell-St. Elias National Park and Preserve," 1984, 91.

[180] Miller, 110-117.

[181] Ibid.

[182] Pilgrim, 88-90.

[183] NOTE: Augusta describes the process of hauling supplies to their summer cabin at Glacier Creek from Dan Creek in May of 1930 in her journal.

[184] James H. Edwards, "Martin Radovan" *Alaskan Sportsman*, (September 1965), 17-18.

[185] *Martin's Dream.*

[186] Hunt, 87.

[187] Pilgrim, 88-90.

[188] Hunt, 87; Miller, 114-117.

[189] *Martin's Dream.*

[190] Edwards, 17-18.

Endnotes

[191] Loy Green, 1994.

[192] *Martin's Dream*.

[193] Loy Green, 1994.

[194] A number of sources describe Martin's Binocular find: Hunt, 87; Edwards, 1965; Loy Green, 1994; as well as his own words from *Martin's Dream*.

[195] Pilgrim, 31.

[196] *Alaska Weekly*, 28 August Correspondence with Sunny Cook, McCarthy Museum President, September 22, 2010. Titles noted in Augusta's Journal.
1931, 8; *Fairbanks Daily News-Miner*, 28 August, 1931; *Alaska Weekly*, 11 September 1931, 1-2.

[197] *Alaska Weekly*, 11 September 1931, 1-2.

[198] *Alaska Weekly*, 11 September 1931, 1-2.

[199] *Fairbanks Daily News-Miner*, 28 August 1931.

[200] Samson Ferreira, Cultural Landscape Inventory, 2009, 26-27.

[201] Archeological Investigation for Site XMC-141, Wrangell Saint Elias National Park and Preserve 94-001.

[202] Ferreira, Cultural Landscape Inventory, 2009, 27.

[203] Loy Green, 1994; *Augusta Radovan's Journal*.

[204] *Augusta Radovan's Journal*.

[205] CLI

[206] Philip S. Smith, "Mineral Industry of Alaska in 1931 and Administrative Report," U.S. Geological Survey, Bulletin 844-A (Washington, D. C., 1933), 1-82.

[207] Letter: From Martin Radovan, McCarthy, Alaska, to USGS, College, Alaska, November 29, 1935. Chititu Mines Co Records, Archives and Special Collections, Consortium Library, University of Alaska Anchorage, Box 1, Folder 1.

[208] Grauman, 49.

[209] Hunt, 84-85.

[210] Grauman, 49-50.

[211] Ibid.

[212] Kennecott Copper Corporation, "Twenty-third Annual Report," 1937, p. 6.

[213] Philip S. Smith, *Mineral Industry of Alaska in 1938*, U.S. Geological Survey, Bulletin 917-A (Washington, D.C.,1939), 87.

[214] Edwards, 18.

[215] *McCarthy Weekly News*, 28 November 1925.

[216] "Charles J. Iverson," *Death Certificate*, Bureau of Vital Statistics, King Country (Washington) Department of Public Health.

[217] "Charles John Iverson," U.S. Census Records, 1930.

[218] *Fairbanks Daily News-Miner*, 27 September 1940.

[219] "Thora F. Iverson," *Death Certificate*, Seattle, King County (Washington) Department of Public Health Vital Statistics Section.

[220] Communication with Valdez Parks and Recreation, June 2010.

[221] NOTE: Both Loy Green and Edwards mention this in their personal accounts of Martin and Augusta.

[222] Letter: Theodore W. Van Zelst to Mrs. Katherine Cesare, 11 June 1985. Martin Radovan Private Collection, Chico, California.

[223] Edwards, 17-18.

[224] Miller, 98-99.

[225] Miller, 98; Letter: Theodore W. Van Zelst, to Mrs. Katherine Cesare, 11 June 1985.

[226] Miller, 98.

[227] W. S. Wright and A. W. Tolonen, "Chitistone Copper Deposits, Chitistone River Area, Alaska," (U.S. Bureau of Mines, 1945).

[228] Ibid.

[229] Ibid.

[230] C. L. Sainsbury, *Geology of the Nelson and Radovan Copper Prospects, Glacier Creek, Alaska*, U.S. Geological Survey, 1951.

[231] Miller, 98.

[232] Miller, 98-99.

[233] Edwards, 17-18.

Endnotes

[234] Ibid.

[235] Letter: Martin Radovan, McCarthy, Alaska to USGS, College, Alaska, November 29, 1935. Chititu Mines Co Records, Archives and Special Collections, Consortium Library, University of Alaska Anchorage, Box 1, Folder 1.

[236] Martin filed his claims at Copper Center on September 13, 1948.

[237] Sainsbury, U.S. Geological Survey (1951).

[238] Ibid.

[239] Ibid.

[240] Logan Hovis and Jeremy Mouat, "Miners, Engineers, and the Transformation of Work in the Western Mining Industry, 1880-1930," in *Technology and Culture* 37, no. 3. (University of Chicago Press, July 1996), 429.

[241] Hovis and Mouat, 429-430.

[242] Edwards, 17-18.

[243] Ibid.

[244] Ibid.

[245] Ibid.

[246] Personal communication with Mark Keogh, whose father, Lynn Keogh, knew Martin in the 1950s.

[247] Casley, "Venerable Sourdough," 1972.

[248] Edwards, 17-18.

[249] NOTE: These items were found by park staff in two of the cabins at Radovan Camp. The original cabin was built around 1929 and the second was built in 1955. NPS, Site Inventory Form, Radovan's Camp.

[250] W.S. Wright and A.W. Tolonen, "Chitistone Copper Deposits, Chitistone River Area, Alaska," (Bureau of Mines, 1945), 1-20.

[251] Kirchhoff, 83.

[252] Robert Spude, Dan Taylor, and Michael Lappen, "Historic Structures Inventory in Wrangell-St. Elias National Park and Preserve," 1984, 133.

[253] Kenny Smith, "Martin Radovan Remembered," *Wrangell-St. Elias News*, November and December 2006.

[254] Kathryn Morse, *The Nature of Gold: An Environmental History of the Klondike Gold Rush* (Seattle: University of Washington Press, 2003), 136.

[255] Loy Green, 1994.

[256] Ibid.

[257] Sainsbury, U.S. Geological Survey, 2.

[258] Alfred L. Ransome and William H. Kerns, *Mineral Yearbook Area Report*, U.S. Bureau of Mines, Vol. III, 1952. 65, 71, 82.

[259] Memo: "Report on the Prospecting Program of the Alaska Copper Company on Claire Creek, Copper River Region, Alaska," from Robert H. Saunders, Associate Mining Engineer, to Leo H. Saarela, Commissioner of Mines, Juneau, Alaska, Department of Mines, Territory of Alaska, 3 March 1952.

[260] Memo: "Report on the Prospecting Program of the Alaska Copper Company on Claire Creek, Copper River Region, Alaska," from Robert H. Saunders, Associate Mining Engineer, to Leo H. Saarela, Commissioner of Mines, Juneau, Alaska, Department of Mines, Territory of Alaska, 3 March 1952.

[261] Saunders, Robert H. "Report on the prospecting of the Alaska Copper Company on Glacier Creek, Copper River region, Alaska," Alaska Dept. of Mines, 1952.

[262] Ibid.

[263] Ibid.

[264] Interview, Emily Aiken Campbell, 18 June 2010.

[265] "Brothers Reunited," 1951; Casley, "Venerable Sourdough," 1972.

[266] NOTE: Martin told the story to *Anchorage Daily Times* reporter Dan Casley at his camp in 1972.

[267] Casley, "Venerable Sourdough," 1972.

[268] "Brothers Reunited," 1951.

[269] Ibid.

[270] Ibid.

[271] W. M. Jasper, "Alaska, Mines, Report of the Commissioner," 13 July 1954.

[272] Ibid.

[273] Ibid.

Endnotes

[274] *Cordova Times*, 10 March 1955.

[275] Ibid; Edwards, 17-18.

[276] Edwards, 17-18.

[277] Edwards, 17-18.

[278] *Cordova Times*, 10 March 1955; Interview, Emily Aiken Campbell, June 2010.

[279] Interview, Emily Aiken Campbell, 18 June 2010.

[280] Martin's Certificate of Naturalization (#7268326) dated March 21, 1969, was "naturalized by the District Court. Issued on March 21, 1969," Martin Radovan Private Collection, Chico, California.

[281] 1956 Radovan, Martin, McCarthy, Glacier Cr., Nizina Dist., McCarthy, Copper lode prospecting, 1 employed (p. 89). Alaska, Mines, Report of the Commissioner, 1956. 1959 Radovan, Martin, McCarthy, Glacier Cr., Nizina Dist., McCarthy, Copper lode prospecting, 1 employed (p. 66). Alaska, DNR, Mines, Report of the Division, 1959. 1960 Radovan, Martin, McCarthy, Glacier Cr., Nizina Dist., McCarthy, Copper lode prospecting, 1 employed (p. 70). Alaska, DNR, Mines, Report of the Division, 1960. 1961 Radovan, Martin, McCarthy, Glacier Cr., Nizina Dist., McCarthy, Copper lode prospecting, 1 employed (p. 97). Alaska, Department of Natural Resources, Mines, Report of the Division, 1961.

[282] Letter: From Martin Radovan, To Cesare Family, 9 January 1964. Martin Radovan Private Collection, Chico, California.

[283] Florida Department of State Division of Corporations, Florida Secretary of State, http://ccfcorp.dos.state.fl.us/search.html.

[284] Agreement between Martin Radovan and Harry B. Cannon Sr., State of Alaska Copper Center Recording District, November 27, 1963. Martin Radovan Private Collection, Chico, California.

[285] Supplemental Agreement, Martin Radovan and Harry B. Cannon Sr., 22 November 1965.

[286] Loy Green, 1994.

[287] Letter, From Martin Radovan, To Katherine Cesare, January 1967. Martin Radovan Private Collection, Chico, California.

[288] Ibid.

[289] Letter: From Martin Radovan, To Radovan Gulch Copper Co, Tampa Florida, circa 1969. Martin Radovan Private Collection, Chico, California.

[290] Ibid.

[291] Letter: Martin Radovan, To Mr. E. B. Anderson, Radovan Gulch Copper Co,. June 5, 1966; Check 170 To Martin Radovan for $5,000 signed by Robert Thomas of the Radovan Gulch Copper Co., June 21, 1966; Check 207 To Martin Radovan for $1,000 signed by Robert Thomas of the Radovan Gulch Copper Co., May 29, 1967; Check 215 To Martin Radovan for $14,000 signed by Robert Thomas of the Radovan Gulch Copper Co., December 22, 1967; Check 221 To Martin Radovan for $10,000 signed by the Radovan Gulch Copper Co,. June 22, 1968; Check 223 To Martin Radovan for $10,000 signed by Robert Thomas of the Radovan Gulch Copper Co., May 21, 1969. *Martin Radovan Collection*, Chico, California.

[292] Letter: From Martin Radovan, To Mr. E .B. Anderson, Radovan Gulch Copper Co., August 4, 1969. Martin Radovan Private Collection, Chico, California.

[293] Letter: From Martin Radovan, To Mr. E. B. Anderson, Radovan Gulch Copper Co., August 25, 1969. Martin Radovan Private Collection, Chico, California.

[294] Letter: From Martin Radovan, To Mr. E. B. Anderson, Radovan Gulch Copper Co., August 25, 1969. Martin Radovan Private Collection, Chico, California.

[295] Letter: From E. B. Anderson, Radovan Gulch Copper Company; To Mr. J. L. MCarrey, Anchorage, Alaska, September 18, 1969. Martin Radovan Private Collection, Chico, California.

[296] Loy Green, 1994.

[297] Ibid.

[298] Florida Department of State Division of Corporations, Radovan Gulch Copper Co., Department of State.

[299] *Fairbanks Daily News-Miner*, 26 May 1970.

[300] Casley, "Venerable Sourdough," 1972.

[301] Ibid.

[302] Tim Larimer, "Geneva Pacific: Belden's Stake in Alaska," Geneva Pacific Corp, Subsidiary of Belden Corporation, 1979.

[303] *Radovan's Dream*.

[304] Photo: Bob Hawkinson (right) and Martin Radovan at Glacier Creek Camp, National Park Service, Anchorage, AK.

[305] Larimer. "Geneva Pacific."

[306] Interview, Gary Green, 10 July 2010.

[307] Casley, "Venerable Sourdough," 1972.

Endnotes

[308] Ibid.

[309] "Geneva Pacific Reaches the Binocular Prospect," Geneva-Pacific Corp. News Release, undated.

[310] "Martin Radovan," Social Security Death Index.

[311] Letter: From TW Van Zelst; To Mrs. Katherine Cesare, 9 July, 1979. Martin Radovan Private Collection, Chico, California.

[312] Department of the Interior News Release, "Cooper Industries Donation in Alaska is Largest in Park Service History," June 1, 1983.

[313] Sykes, "Martin Radovan: Prospector," unpublished article for Geneva Pacific dated May 8, 1980.

[314] Letter: From Phil R. Holdsworth, To Mrs. Catherine Cesare, 20July 1975. Martin Radovan Private Collection, Chico, California.

[315] Quoted by Langdon and Dodson in "Radovan Camp," Site Inventory Form, NPS, 1994.

[316] Ibid.

[317] Letter: From Theodore W. Van Zelst, From Mrs. Cesare, November 15, 1983. Martin Radovan Private Collection, Chico, California.

[318] Loy Green, 1994.

[319] "Martin F. Radovan Services Today," *Delano Record*, 24 June 1975, 3.

[320] Though there are many monographs that might be cited, an important book on this topic is *The Women's West*, edited by Susan Armitage and Elizabeth Jameson (Norman: University of Oklahoma Press, 1987).

[321] NOTE: Richard White makes a compelling argument that people who work in nature tend to know it better than those who recreate or play in it. Richard White, "'Are You an Environmentalist or Do You Work for a Living?': Work and Nature," in *Uncommon Ground: Rethinking the Human Place in Nature*, ed. William Cronon. (New York: W.W. Norton & Company, 1996), 171-185.

[322] *Martin's Dream*.

[323] Ibid.

[324] Langdon and Dodson.

[325] Edwards, 17-18.